D1171107

Mokele-mbembe

FACT OR FICTION?

CREATURE SCENE INVESTIGATION

Mokele-mbembe

FACT OR FICTION?

Rick Emmer

CHELSEA HOUSE
PUBLISHERS
An imprint of Infobase Publishing

MOKELE-MBEMBE: FACT OR FICTION?

Chelsea House
An imprint of Infobase Publishing
132 West 31st Street
New York NY 10001

Library of Congress Cataloging-in-Publication Data
Emmer, Rick.
  Mokele-mbembe: fact or fiction? / Rick Emmer.
    p. cm. — (Creature scene investigation)
  Includes bibliographical references and index.
  ISBN 978-0-7910-9781-6 (hardcover)
  1. Mokele-mbembe—Juvenile literature. I. Title. II. Series.
  QL89.2.M58E46 2010
  001.944—dc22   2009011466

Chelsea House books are available at special discounts when purchased in bulk quantities for businesses, associations, institutions, or sales promotions. Please call our Special Sales Department in New York at (212) 967-8800 or (800) 322-8755.

You can find Chelsea House on the World Wide Web at http://www.chelseahouse.com.

Text design by James Scotto-Lavino, Erik Lindstrom
Cover design by Takeshi Takahashi
Composition by EJB Publishing Services
Cover printed by Bang Printing, Brainerd, Minn.
Book printed and bound by Bang Printing, Brainerd, Minn.
Date Printed: January 2010
Printed in the United States of America

Printed in the United States of America

10 9 8 7 6 5 4 3 2 1

CONTENTS

PREFACE

Welcome to Creature Scene Investigation: The Science of Cryptozoology, the series devoted to the science of **cryptozoology**. Bernard Heuvelmans, a French scientist, invented that word 50 years ago. It is a combination of the words *kryptos* (Greek for "hidden") and *zoology*, the scientific study of animals. So, cryptozoology is the study of "hidden" animals, or **cryptids**, which are animals that some people believe may exist, even though it is not yet proven.

Just how does a person prove that a particular cryptid exists? Dedicated cryptozoologists (the scientists who study cryptozoology) follow a long, two-step process as they search for cryptids. First, they gather as much information about their animal as they can. The most important sources of information are people who live near where the cryptid supposedly lives. These people are most familiar with the animal and the stories about it. So, for example, if cryptozoologists want to find out about the Loch Ness Monster, they must ask the people who live around Loch Ness, a lake in Scotland where the monster was sighted. If they want to learn about Bigfoot, they should talk to people who found its footprints or took its photo.

A cryptozoologist carefully examines all of this information. This is important because it helps the scientist identify and rule out some stories that might be mistakes or lies. The remaining information can then be used to produce a clear scientific description of the cryptid in question. It might even lead to solid proof that the cryptid exists.

Second, a cryptozoologist takes the results of his or her research and goes into the field to look for solid evidence that the cryptid really exists. The best possible evidence would be an actual **specimen**—maybe even a live one. Short of that, a combination of good videos, photographs, footprints, body parts (bones and teeth, for example), and other clues can make a strong case for a cryptid's existence.

In this way, the science of cryptozoology is a lot like **forensics**, the science made famous by all of those crime investigation shows on TV. The goal of forensics detectives is to use the evidence they find to catch a criminal. The goal of cryptozoologists is to catch a cryptid—or at least to find solid evidence that it really exists.

Some cryptids have become world-famous. The most famous ones of all are probably the legendary Loch Ness Monster of Scotland and the apelike Bigfoot of the United States. There are many other cryptids out there, too. At least, some people think so.

This series explores the legends and lore—the facts and the fiction—behind the most popular of all of the cryptids: the gigantic shark known as Megalodon, Kraken the monster squid, an African dinosaur called Mokele-mbembe, the Loch Ness Monster, and Bigfoot. This series also takes a look at some lesser-known but equally fascinating cryptids from around the world:

- the mysterious, blood-sucking Chupacabras, or "goat sucker," from the Caribbean, Mexico, and South America
- the Sucuriju, a giant anaconda snake from South America
- Megalania, the gigantic monitor lizard from Australia
- the Ropen and Kongamato, prehistoric flying reptiles from Africa and the island of New Guinea
- the thylacine, or Tasmanian wolf, from the island of Tasmania

- the Ri, a mermaidlike creature from the waters of New Guinea
- the thunderbird, a giant vulture from western North America

Some cryptids, such as dinosaurs like Mokele-mbembe, are animals already known to science. These animals are thought to have become extinct. Some people, however, believe that these animals are still alive in lands that are difficult for most humans to reach. Other cryptids, such as the giant anaconda snake, are simply unusually large (or, in some cases, unusually small) versions of modern animals. And yet other cryptids, such as the Chupacabras, appear to be animals right out of a science fiction movie, totally unlike anything known to modern science.

As cryptozoologists search for these unusual animals, they keep in mind a couple of slogans. The first is, "If it sounds too good to be true, it probably isn't true." The second is, "Absence of proof is not proof of absence." The meaning of these slogans will become clear as you observe how crypto-zoologists analyze and interpret the evidence they gather in their search for these awesome animals.

ONE WHO STOPS THE FLOW OF RIVERS

*The Mokele-mbembe is undoubtedly the zoo-
logical craze of the 1980s. Just possibly it could
become the greatest zoological discovery of the
twentieth century—indeed of any century.*

—Bernard Heuvelmans,
in Roy P. Mackal's *A Living Dinosaur*

*A*ccording to African legend, a bloody war once raged
in the heart of the central African rain forest. A band
of **pygmies** who were fleeing the mayhem came upon the
roiling waters of a fast-flowing river, too dangerous to cross.
As they pondered what to do, a great beast suddenly rose

from the watery depths. With its long tail, hulking back, stretched-out neck, and sturdy legs, the beast became a living bridge, spanning the river from shore to shore. The pygmies nimbly clambered up the creature's tail, scrambled across its broad back, and scampered down its long neck to safety on the other side of the river.

Encounters with this awesome creature weren't always so pleasant. If you stood too close to the spot where the colossal beast erupted from the water, chances were you would be knocked over by the resulting wave and then sucked under and drowned as the water sloshed back into the deep river. Also, the beast didn't like sharing its river with anyone else. It drove away any hippos, elephants, and crocodiles that ventured too close, and it smashed any fishing boat that came into view, killing—but never eating—every person on board.

The pygmy and **Bantu** inhabitants of the African rain forest have a name for this monster, which they claim still haunts the lakes and rivers of the vast Likouala Swamp. This swamp is located in the People's Republic of the Congo—not to be confused with the neighboring Democratic Republic of the Congo. The two nations are separated by the mighty Congo River, which flows in a south-southwesterly direction along the eastern border of the People's Republic of the Congo.

In the language of the Bantu, this monster is called Mokele-mbembe (pronounced "mo-kay-lee mmmbem-bee"), which means "one who stops the flow of rivers," and it has created quite a stir in the cryptozoological community. That's because this beast isn't any run-of-the-mill swamp monster. The way the natives describe it, there's only one type of animal this creature resembles. With its long tail, equally long neck, bulky body, and stout legs, Mokele-mbembe sounds just like a creature known as a **sauropod**. The problem is, sauropods are a type of **dinosaur**. Virtually all **paleontologists** believe that the last of the dinosaurs became extinct at the end of the **Cretaceous Period**, around 65 million

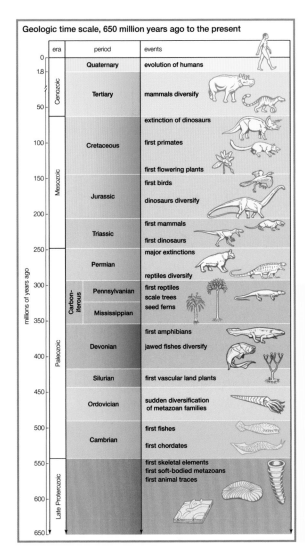

Geologic time scale, 650 million years ago to the present

The geologic time scale divides and subdivides the 4.5 billion years of Earth's history into smaller and smaller units of time. The fossil record indicates that sauropods existed from the end of the Triassic Period to the end of the Cretaceous Period.

years ago. The only modern-day descendants of dinosaurs are thought to be feathered fliers: the birds. Clearly, Mokele-mbembe is no bird.

MOKELE-MBEMBE: FACT OR FANCY?

As is typical in the world of cryptozoology, there is much more to the Mokele-mbembe phenomenon than meets—or in this case, doesn't meet—the eye. Not only does this possibly-never-seen-by-Western-scientists creature supposedly exist both in flesh and blood, it is said to exist in mind and spirit as well. So to really appreciate what Mokele-mbembe is all about, it is important to take a look at the supernatural as well as the natural aspects of what may be the most complicated of all cryptids.

A World of Fetishes and Folk Healers

Pygmy and Bantu cultures revolve around the concept of **animism**, the belief that every object in the natural world is inhabited by a supernatural spirit or soul. According to this belief, every object, whether it's a tree, river, mountain, flower, ant—or even Mokele-mbembe—was once part of an **immortal**, godlike being. This means that each and every one of these objects is in some sense alive and needs to be treated with respect.

Visitors to central and western Africa are often reminded of this animist culture by the abundance of **fetishes.** Fetishes are objects such as pebbles; seeds; bits of hair, skin, or claws of animals; or other items that the native people carry around with them or keep in their homes. The people believe that within each of these seemingly ordinary objects dwells a soul or spirit. This spirit is of special significance to its owner and may possess supernatural powers.

It is not uncommon for natives to speak or pray to their fetish, seeking advice, consolation, or understanding. Each village typically has a resident **folk healer** (referred to by tourists and other outsiders as a "witch doctor"). Healers have received extensive training in divining, or communicating with spirits; they communicate with spirits in fetishes as well as those residing in the surrounding rain forest. In addition, healers learn how to make use of the vast natural pharmacy contained within the rain forest, concocting remedies to treat everything from scorpion stings to headaches. Modern medical science pooh-poohs many of these folk remedies, but chemicals derived from some of the medicinal plants and animal parts have been shown to be effective in treating certain ailments.

Of all the spirits that reside in the rain forest, that of Mokele-mbembe is one of the most revered. In fact, Mokele-mbembe is often looked upon as being some sort of powerful rain forest god. More than one foreign adventurer seeking this mysterious creature has had to first seek the blessing of the local folk healer before being allowed to enter the swampland where Mokele-mbembe hides.

As if this secretive creature weren't already mysterious enough, many natives who claim to have seen it are afraid to talk about it. They fear that the spirit of Mokele-mbembe will become angry and kill them if they do so. This supernatural aspect of Mokele-mbembe is so important to the natives that some **skeptics** suspect that the creature may be a purely mythological beast, right up there with unicorns and dragons.

Nevertheless, some natives have talked to outsiders about Mokele-mbembe. As is typical with eyewitness descriptions of unknown animals, the descriptions vary from witness to witness. The animal described, however, is, by and large, just the animal you would expect to find if a living, breathing sauropod dinosaur were roaming the remote waters of the great Likouala Swamp.

Portrait of a Modern-Day Sauropod

In typical sauropod fashion, Mokele-mbembe reportedly possesses a long, muscular, tapering tail; a broad, bulky body supported by sturdy elephantine legs; a long, slender neck; and a tiny head. According to some pygmies, the beast has blood-red eyes and rusty red skin covered with very short

Descriptions of Mokele-mbembe fit the appearance of the long-necked, small-headed sauropods. An artist's depiction of *Diplodocus*, a type of sauropod, is seen here.

hair. Other witnesses describe a creature with smooth, black or brown skin that is hairless and sometimes scaly looking. Witnesses sometimes describe a structure at the back of the head and neck that sounds a bit like a horse's mane or a rooster's comb.

Mokele-mbembe is usually described as larger than a hippopotamus but smaller than an elephant. That's pretty small by sauropod standards, where giants such as *Brachiosaurus* (the dinosaur that sneezed in Lex Murphy's face in the 1993 movie *Jurassic Park*) would have towered over even the biggest elephant. Mokele-mbembe, however, would still be one of the largest land animals on Earth today.

Some people say Mokele-mbembe makes noises. A wide range of vocalizations has been reported: everything from whispers to hisses to deafening roars. Mokele-mbembe is almost exclusively aquatic, spending most of its time in shallow water fringing the shores of rivers and lakes located in the vast Likouala Swamp, which is in the northeastern corner of the People's Republic of the Congo.

Finally, one thing that virtually all witnesses agree upon is that Mokele-mbembe eats plants. Mokele-mbembe is consistently described as **herbivorous**, dining exclusively on leaves and fruit, particularly the molombo (also spelled malombo), an apple-sized fruit produced by a vine that commonly grows along the edges of rivers and lakes that the beast frequents.

THE LIKOUALA SWAMP
Central Africa is home to one of the world's grandest rain forests. Straddling the equator, the bulk of the African rain forest runs through the countries of Cameroon, Equatorial Guinea, and Gabon along the Atlantic coast. It extends eastward in a band 300 miles (480 km) wide, through the People's Republic of the Congo, the Central African Republic, and the Democratic Republic of the Congo, for more than 1,200 miles (1,920 kilometers). Although a narrow strip of **montane rain forest** (rain forest at an elevation greater than 4,000 feet [1,200 meters] above sea level) runs along the eastern border of the Democratic Republic of the Congo, the bulk of the African rain forest is **lowland rain forest** (elevation less than 4,000 feet), much of which is contained within a vast low-lying region known as the Congo Basin. Eight hundred thousand square miles (2.1 million square km) in area, it is as large as the state of Alaska. It is within this basin that Mokele-mbembe is said to make its home.

Mokele-mbembe's Lair
The majority of Mokele-mbembe sightings have occurred in the Likouala Swamp. Covering about 55,000 square miles (140,000 square km), this vast wetland appears at first glance

Africa's Congo Basin

The Congo Basin is located in central Africa and extends eastward from the Atlantic coast in a band 300 miles (480 km) wide, for approximately 1,200 miles (1,920 km).

to be impenetrable to anything other than snakes, spiders, and disease-carrying flies and mosquitoes. There are, however, large sections of relatively dry land that emerge above the sopping wet swamp, providing habitat for many land animals, including elephants, tortoises, lizards, birds, leopards, monkeys, chimpanzees, and gorillas.

There are also several lakes in the Likouala region. One in particular, Lake Tele (also spelled Lake Telle, Lake Télé, and

Lac Tele), seems to be a Mokele-mbembe magnet. According to local pygmy and Bantu tribes, Mokele-mbembe frequents the shallow near-shore waters of Lake Tele, where the water is less than 6 feet (2 m) deep. While its legs and most of its body stay submerged and hidden from view in the dark-brown water, the animal stretches its long neck skyward to feed on the plentiful overhanging vegetation.

The Real "Lost World"?

When Professor Challenger led his expedition to a volcanic plateau in the South American rain forest in Arthur Conan Doyle's novel *The Lost World*, it was as though time had stood still since the **Mesozoic Era**, the Age of Dinosaurs. Dinosaurs walked on the land, **pterodactyls** flew in the air, and **plesiosaurs** swam in the water. The jungle was populated with ancient plants as well. To modern real-life adventurers visiting Lake Tele and the surrounding rain forest in the Likouala Swamp, the impression is the same. Granted, there are no plesiosaurs, flying reptiles, or dinosaurs—except, perhaps, for the subject of this book—but much of the vegetation (tree ferns, **cycads**, and the like) looks like it came right out of the Cretaceous Period. As paleontologist Christine Janis explains, a sauropod survivor from the Cretaceous would feel right at home here:

> If there *is* some undescribed large animal in the Likouala swamps, what is the likelihood that it could be a surviving sauropod—presumably one of a small, surviving population? I do not consider this [to be] highly probable. But, given the fact that the Congolese swamp forests and vegetation have been virtually undisturbed—at least in terms of latitudinal position in the equatorial zone—since the end of

(continues on page 20)

LET'S GET TECHNICAL: PLATE TECTONICS

*I*f you could slice Earth in half, you would find that it has a layered structure resembling a hard-boiled egg. In the center, corresponding to the egg yolk, is Earth's incredibly hot **core**, which is composed mainly of the metals iron and nickel. Surrounding the core is the **mantle**—the egg white. The deeper portion of the mantle, the **asthenosphere**, is composed of molten rock. In contrast, the relatively thin upper portion of the mantle is very stiff and rigid, and—along with Earth's rocky surface, or **crust** (the egg shell)—comprises the **lithosphere**, which floats on the asthenosphere. There are two types of crust: the relatively thick continental crust, which forms the continents, and the much thinner but denser oceanic crust, which forms the floor of the world's oceans.

According to the theory of plate tectonics, the lithosphere is composed of several large pieces, or plates, which move very slowly across the top of the asthenosphere. Over millions of years, the plates slowly bump into and grind past each other, producing earthquakes, volcanoes, and mountain ranges.

All interactions between plates occur along their edges, or boundaries, where one of three things may happen. In some places the plates move away, or diverge, from each other, leaving a gap in the middle. Such boundaries are called **divergent boundaries.** In other places, the plates converge, or move toward each other, creating **convergent boundaries.** Along the third type of boundary, the plates slide and scrape past each other, a process that deforms their edges and creates **transform boundaries**.

The Mid-Atlantic Ridge, an underwater mountain range that snakes its way along the floor of the Atlantic Ocean, is an example of a divergent boundary. It separates the South American, Caribbean, and North American plates to the west from the Eurasian and African plates to the east. As these plates move apart, molten rock, or magma, rises from the asthenosphere to fill in the widening gap. As the magma cools and solidifies, it piles up and forms the mountains that make up the Mid-Atlantic Ridge. This material gradually spreads out to the east and west in a process called **seafloor spreading**. The result is a gradual widening of the Atlantic Ocean basin.

A well-known convergent boundary is found along the west coast of South America. Here, the east-moving Nazca plate is converging with the west-moving South American plate. Because the Nazca plate is denser than the South American plate, it bends down and slides beneath the South American plate in a process called **subduction**. This creates the Peru-Chile Trench, which runs along the ocean floor off the western coast of South America. Several miles inland from the trench, hot magma rises to the surface, forming a string of volcanoes that runs along the west coast of South America. These volcanoes form the backbone of the Andes Mountains.

California's San Andreas Fault is probably the best-known transform boundary. Here, the Pacific plate is moving toward the northwest. As its eastern edge slides in herky-jerky fashion along the western edge of the North American plate, the result is earthquakes that pose a constant threat to residents of the West Coast.

The African plate is unusual in that it is surrounded on three sides (to the west, south, and east) by relatively weak divergent boundaries and to the north by the much larger Eurasian plate. The forces created by the diverging eastern and western boundaries cancel each other out, and the northern push by the southern boundary is not powerful enough to shove the huge Eurasian plate out of the way. As a result, the African plate has been stuck where it is since the end of the Cretaceous Period.

(continued from page 17)

the Cretaceous, the fact that sauropods survived in this region at least up until this time, and the fact that there has been no fossil record available from the Central African equatorial region since the end of the Cretaceous, I am forced to conclude that, if there was anywhere on earth where sauropods *might* have survived until recent times, this would be the most likely place.

Noted cryptozoologist Roy P. Mackal echoes Janis's sentiment. "Again, I should emphasize that the Likouala region has remained relatively unchanged since the Cretaceous Period," he says. "No mountain formation or extensive **inundation** has occurred and the climate has been stable for millions of years. It is ideally suited for the survival of a **relict** species." Unlike the other continents, which through the process of **plate tectonics** have slowly changed their position relative to the Earth's equator since the Cretaceous Period, Africa has pretty much stayed put. As a result, the Congo Basin has stayed close to the equator for the duration. Time obviously didn't stand still, but Africa sure did. Because of this, the climate of the Congo Basin hasn't changed as much as it has on the other continents, some of whose **latitudinal position** (distance north or south of the equator) has changed by hundreds or even thousands of miles, causing significant changes in climate.

Having gathered information about the appearance and lifestyle of Mokele-mbembe, the creature's habitat, and its relation to the people of the Congo region, this investigation is ready to roll. Since Mokele-mbembe seems to resemble a sauropod dinosaur more than anything else, it's clear that the next stage of our investigation must be to find out what is known about sauropod biology. That way,

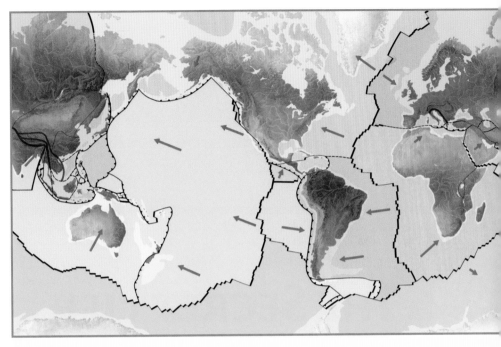

Earth's lithosphere is divided into several tectonic plates that bump into and grind past each other, creating earthquakes, volcanoes, and mountain ranges in the process.

it will be possible to examine and evaluate the details of Mokele-mbembe sightings that have been reported over the years. Even though scientists have no live specimens to go by—at least not yet—they have learned quite a bit about the **anatomy** and behavior of sauropods by studying their fossil remains. It's time to take a look at just what paleontologists have discovered.

The Secret Life
of Sauropods

*J*ust what is a dinosaur, anyway? If you think it's a reptile, you're right. If you think it's a supersized lizard, you're wrong. Although many dinosaurs look superficially like gigantic lizards, the structure of certain parts of their skeletons, especially the joint where the upper leg bone (**femur**) attaches to the hip, or **pelvis**, clearly indicate that they are not very closely related to lizards. The legs of a lizard splay out to the sides. As a result, when a lizard moves, it barely raises its belly off the ground. Dinosaur legs, on the other hand, are slung under the body in a nearly vertical position—just like they are in their modern descendants, the birds. Believe it or not, birds, including the tiniest hummingbird, are actually descendants of a diminutive cousin of the largest carnivore to ever walk the land, *Tyrannosaurus rex*.

Saurolophus, a duck-billed dinosaur (*top*), and *Triceratops*, a horned dinosaur (*bottom*), were ornithischians, or "bird-hipped" dinosaurs.

Dinosaurs are **archosaurs**, a group of reptiles that also includes pterodactyls and crocodilians (alligators and crocodiles). Archosaurs first appeared in the Triassic Period, more than 200 million years ago. Pterodactyls died out with the dinosaurs at the end of the Cretaceous Period. Crocodilians and birds are the only archosaurs known to have survived to modern times.

Two types of dinosaur arose from the ancestral archosaurs. They differ in the shape and arrangement of the bones of the pelvis. In the **ornithischians**, or "bird-hipped" dinosaurs, the pelvis looks a bit like that of modern birds. The best-known members of this group are the duck-billed dinosaurs and the armored dinosaurs, such as spike-tailed *Stegosaurus*, club-tailed *Ankylosaurus*, and three-horned *Triceratops*. All of the ornithischians were **herbivores**.

The **saurischians**, or "lizard-hipped" dinosaurs, had a pelvis that looked a bit like that of modern-day lizards. Two very different types of dinosaur made up this group. The first were the **theropods**. These were voracious, **bipedal** (two-legged) predators such as *T. rex*, *Allosaurus*, and *Velociraptor*—the stuff that nightmares and smash-hit sci-fi movies are made of. The second were the sauropods, gigantic **quadrupedal** (four-legged), long-necked plant-eaters such as the 80-ton (72,730-kg) *Sauroposeidon* and its little cousin *Brachiosaurus* (weighing in at a mere 50 tons [45,450 kg]). Also included in this group was the slender but elongated 90-foot (27-m) *Diplodocus* and, if the people of the Likouala Swamp are correct, a much smaller beast by the name of Mokele-mbembe.

The sauropods were true survivors. Among the first dinosaurs to evolve, they managed to survive to the very end of the Age of the Dinosaurs. If we can discover the secret to their success, we may be able to determine the likelihood of one member of their clan beating the odds and surviving to modern times.

THE BIOLOGY OF SAUROPODS

Compared with other dinosaurs, sauropods appear rather plain-looking and unimpressive. They lack the showy frills (bony growths extending from the back of the skull down toward the neck), spikes, and horns of the ornithischians, as

The theropod *Tyrannosaurus* (*top*) and the sauropod *Brachiosaurus* (*bottom*) were saurischians, or "lizard-hipped" dinosaurs.

well as the fearsome teeth and claws of the theropod saurischians. Yet, one thing about sauropods makes them stand out from all the other dinosaurs: their size.

It can be said without exaggeration that the largest of the sauropods stood head and shoulders above—way above—all other animals, past or present. Consider this: The largest land mammal on Earth today is the bull (male) African elephant, which can tip the scales at 6.5 tons (5,900 kg). That means that 80-ton *Sauroposeidon* weighed as much as 12 bull elephants. Paleontologists have recently uncovered fossils of another sauropod that may have weighed close to 100 tons (91,000 kg). This matches the weight of the blue whale, the largest animal that ever lived. By growing to gigantic size, these sauropods were virtually immune to attack from all but the biggest, baddest theropods.

Not all sauropods had such a size advantage. In fact, the smallest species, at only 1.5 tons (1,360 kg), were only as big as a medium-sized rhinoceros. How these smaller species held their own against predators is not known. Fossilized footprint tracks indicate that sauropods traveled in herds, so perhaps smaller species of sauropod simply traveled in groups large enough to withstand the occasional loss of one of their herd to hungry predators, much as herds of zebra and wildebeest survive the attacks of lions. As the old saying goes, "There is safety in numbers."

What might seem to be an even bigger—and certainly more basic—puzzle is how these small-headed, big-bodied animals managed to eat enough food to stay alive. In this case, however, the fossil record provides a pretty definite answer.

The Perpetual-Munching Machine

The head of all sauropods was downright puny compared with the size of the body. How could such a small head chew up enough vegetation to feed such a bulky animal? The sauropods solved this puzzle by not chewing at all. In fact, even if they wanted to chew their food, they couldn't. Their teeth were shaped like little pegs or chisels, making them ill-suited for mashing up tough, fibrous plant material. Those teeth, however, were perfectly designed to pluck and strip leaves, stems, and fruits off of trees and bushes.

As soon as these tasty morsels were nabbed, they were immediately swallowed down the long neck and deposited in a muscular sac called the **gizzard**. Inside the gizzard were several small stones that the animal had previously

Diplodocus and other sauropods had chisel-like teeth at the front of the jaw. These teeth were used to strip leaves off of vegetation. This *Diplodocus* skull from the Jurassic Period was found in Wyoming.

swallowed. Here was where the sauropod's food was "chewed." As the gizzard muscles contracted, they squished, mashed, and pulverized the ingested plant material against the stones. These gizzard stones, or **gastroliths**, are typically smooth and rounded, like river pebbles, as a result of rubbing against each other while grinding up the sauropod's food.

Paleontologists know for a fact that these stones are gastroliths: They have found piles of these smooth stones along with the fossilized ribs of many sauropods. One very special fossilized specimen of the African sauropod *Massospondylus* actually contained the fossilized muscular lining of the gizzard itself along with the stones, proving that the stones were indeed gastroliths.

Because the gizzard did the "chewing," a sauropod could spend all its feeding time constantly gathering food. This is where the long neck came into play. The sauropod could stand still and flex its neck back and forth, up and down, like a vacuum cleaner hose, continuously stripping away all the edible vegetation within the animal's **feeding envelope**, the area within reach of its searching jaws. This method of simultaneously harvesting and processing food must have been very efficient. Otherwise, the small-headed sauropods would not have flourished from the end of the Triassic to the end of the Cretaceous—a span of approximately 150 million years.

Studying Neck Movement

Just how flexible was the sauropod neck? Until recently, most paleontologists imagined that the typical sauropod neck was quite flexible, able to curl wide to the left and right, bend down to the ground, and extend upward in a nearly vertical, giraffelike pose, providing a very large feeding envelope. New computer simulations of sauropod neck movement, designed by computer expert Kent Stevens and paleontologist Michael Parrish, suggest otherwise.

Stevens and Parrish's DinoMorph computer program predicted the range of motion of the necks of two well-known sauropods, *Diplodocus* and *Apatosaurus* (formerly known as *Brontosaurus*). Starting from a neutral position, where the neck **vertebrae** were snugged up against one another, with no gaps at the sides, top, or bottom between neighboring vertebrae, both dinosaurs' long necks angled slightly downward, positioning the head very close to the ground. The necks were relatively inflexible. They couldn't bend very far in any direction before the vertebrae crunched against one other. For example, *Diplodocus*, which stood 9 feet (2.7 m) tall at the shoulder and had a neck 20 feet (6 m) long, would have been able to reach tree branches nearly 30 feet (9 m) high if its neck were as flexible as a giraffe's. DinoMorph, however, predicted that *Diplodocus* could raise its head only 13 feet (4 m) above the ground, although it could lower its head 5 feet (1.5 m) below ground level. These intriguing results indicate that *Diplodocus* did not browse high in the treetops. Instead, it more likely grazed on vegetation at or near ground level, and may actually have harvested underwater plants growing near the shore of rivers and lakes.

This ground-level feeding envelope fits nicely with *Diplodocus*'s overall posture. Its front legs were shorter than its back legs, so the front of its body pointed downward. This, along with its downward-pointing neck, would have made *Diplodocus* an especially efficient grazer of low-lying vegetation. Most sauropods had hind legs that were longer than their front legs. The only exceptions were *Brachiosaurus* and a few close relatives, whose front legs were slightly longer than their back legs, and whose necks were designed to be held giraffelike, high in the air, enabling these giants to feed on vegetation high up in the trees.

It's useful to know the relative lengths of the front and hind legs of sauropods, as this information helps paleontologists to determine and compare the posture and feeding habits of different species. The easiest way to do this is to calculate the leg-length ratio:

$$\text{Leg-length ratio} = \frac{\text{length of foreleg}}{\text{length of hind leg}}$$

Notice that if the forelegs and hind legs are of equal length, the leg-length ratio equals 1.0. A ratio greater than 1.0 means the forelegs were longer than the hind legs. (The leg length ratio for *Brachiosaurus* is 1.01.) A ratio less than 1.0 means that the hind legs were longer than the forelegs, meaning that the animal's hips were higher off the ground than its shoulders. The leg-length ratio for the African sauropod *Dicraeosaurus*, a relative of *Diplodocus*, was 0.64, which means that its hips were considerably higher than its shoulders.

Dicraeosaurus was an unusual animal, not just for its low leg-length ratio. There is one bizarre feature about this dinosaur that sets it apart from all other known African sauropods: a structure on the back of the neck that sounds similar to the horse's mane or cockscomb some eyewitnesses have seen on Mokele-mbembe. It's a good idea to take a closer look at this shared feature, as some cryptozoologists feel that this has to be more than just a coincidence. If Mokele-mbembe really does exist, it's quite possible that it is a descendant of *Dicraeosaurus*.

DICRAEOSAURIDS: ANCESTORS TO MOKELE-MBEMBE?

Paleontologists recognize more than 120 distinct species of sauropod. Of these, only three species are known to have a structure that, in a live animal, might have looked like a substantial mane or crest on the back of the neck. These species are distributed between two closely related **genera** (the plural of **genus**) that are the sole members of the **taxonomic** family of sauropods known as **Dicraeosauridae**. As you might have guessed, *Dicraeosaurus*, which claims two of those species, is one of those genera. The structure these species possess is the result of an unusual feature of their neck vertebrae.

The Dinosaur with a 'Do

Artists' illustrations of sauropods typically show animals with naked skin—no adornments whatsoever. That type of image, however, may not be appropriate for dicraeosaurids. *Dicraeosaurus* had a pair of long projections, called **neural spines**, that stuck up from the top of each neck

Dicraeosaurus (*top*) had long neural spines atop its vertebrae. They may have stuck out the back of the neck, giving the appearance of a crest. If there were a membrane stretched between the spines, the crest would look like a much smaller version of the "sail" on the back of the ancient reptile *Dimetrodon* (*bottom*).

vertebra. These spines were several inches long, and some paleontologists believe that the spines actually poked out of the back of the neck. It is possible that skin stretched between the spines in a manner similar to what is seen in the ancient sail-backed reptile *Dimetrodon*. If that is the case, the structure might look something like the mane, crest, or cockscomb described by witnesses.

The fact that Mokele-mbembe is only sometimes described as having a crest or mane might be a result of **sexual dimorphism**. The crest might be more highly developed and colorful and therefore more noticeable in males, where it would function as a display to intimidate rival males and/or attract females—a dinosaurian version of a peacock's tail.

Dinosaur Dwarfs

One fact about *Dicraeosaurus* doesn't quite fit with the descriptions of Mokele-mbembe: its size. *Dicraeosaurus* was a medium-sized sauropod, growing to 40 feet (12 m) or more in length. This is quite a bit larger than Mokele-mbembe, which is usually estimated to be somewhere between 20 and 25 feet (6–8 m) long. Yet, there is a totally natural way to explain this significant size difference: the phenomenon known as **insular dwarfism**. Insular dwarfism is a condition in which small islands with limited resources—particularly food and water—are inhabited by animals smaller than, but otherwise the same as, their mainland counterparts.

What does insular dwarfism have to do with Mokele-mbembe? After all, this animal is said to live in the African rain forest, not on an island. As it turns out, the African rain forest hasn't always been as vast as it is today. In the time since the end of the Cretaceous Period, the African rain forest has repeatedly shrunk and expanded in response to changes in climate triggered by, of all things, ice ages, the most recent one occurring between 18,000 and 10,000 years ago.

While temperatures in equatorial Africa were not affected all that much by the buildup of glaciers at the poles (temperatures near the equator dropped only a few degrees), rainfall patterns changed appreciably. Much less rain fell in central Africa during each ice age. As a result, the rain forest shrank to a tiny fraction of its original expanse, leaving only a few isolated pockets, or **refuges**, of moist rain forest habitat surrounded by desert. Today, one can actually find a layer of desert sand beneath the rain forest floor in the Congo Basin, which is proof of the dry climate that existed during the last ice age. The post-Cretaceous African rain forest was clearly not the unchanging world that many Mokele-mbembe enthusiasts envision.

Rain forest animals unable to survive in the encroaching desert would have ended up as refugees, living on the limited resources of rain forest "islands" surrounded by dry "oceans" of sand. Large herbivores such as sauropods would have been particularly hard-pressed to find enough food in such a situation. A downsized, insular dwarf sauropod might have evolved as a result.

The fossil record for *Dicraeosaurus* is limited to the Jurassic Period. So, if a dwarf dicraeosaurid Mokele-mbembe did exist—at this stage of the game, an admittedly big "if"—it would almost certainly be a more recent species. As luck would have it, such a species was recently discovered.

Amargasaurus: Dicraeosaurus's Cousin

The second dicraeosaurid genus goes by the name of *Amargasaurus*. Discovered in 1991, this more recent relative of *Dicraeosaurus* hails from the Cretaceous Period. It also had elongated neural spines (longer even than those of *Dicraeosaurus*), and at about 20 to 30 feet (6.2–9.1 m) long, it was the same size as Mokele-mbembe. It would seem a pretty good match, except for one thing: *Amargasaurus* lived in South America. Thanks to plate tectonics, however, that seemingly major problem is no problem at all.

During most of the Jurassic Period, South America and Africa lay right next to each other and formed part of a super-huge continent called **Gondwana**. In the early Cretaceous Period, South America and Africa began to slowly drift apart. Since *Dicraeosaurus* fossils have been found in the African country of Tanzania, and *Amargasaurus* fossils have been found in the South American country of Argentina, it is likely that dicraeosaurids originated in Africa and then expanded their range westward into the future South America.

Perhaps a dicraeosaurid such as *Amargasaurus* inhabited both sides of the divergent boundary that eventually developed into the Mid-Atlantic Ridge. The population of sauropods west of the ridge would have ended up in South America,

LET'S GET TECHNICAL: INSULAR DWARFISM

Animals inhabiting islands are often smaller than their counterparts on the mainland, a phenomenon known as insular dwarfism. (The term *insular* means "of an island.") For example, a tiny variety of elephant once inhabited the Mediterranean island of Cyprus. Known as the Cyprus dwarf elephant, this animal reached an adult weight of only 440 pounds (200 kg), a fraction of the weight of its ancestor, a huge species of **mammoth** (a type of prehistoric elephant) that weighed several tons.

Tigers come in a variety of sizes, too. The largest of all tigers is the 500-pound (227-kg) Bengal tiger of India. The smaller Sumatran tiger, from the island of Sumatra, only reaches 300 pounds (136 kg). Smaller still, the extinct Bali tiger from the Indonesian island of Bali weighed only 200 pounds (91 kg). The Bali tiger was driven to extinction by humans. The last one was shot and killed in 1937.

Dinosaurs also came in dwarf varieties. What may be the most famous of all were 11 specimens of a diminutive sauropod recently discovered in northern Germany. Named *Europasaurus*, these sauropods while the population to the east would have remained in Africa. If that African population somehow managed to avoid the extinction suffered by all the other dinosaurs at the end of the Cretaceous Period, it could have survived in the Congo Basin right up to modern times, been discovered by humans, and given the majestic moniker Mokele-mbembe.

A Submerged Sauropod?

Not everything about dicraeosaurids is a perfect match to Mokele-mbembe. The structure of the vertebrae of dicraeo-saurids suggests that their neck, like that of *Diplodocus*,

were closely related to *Brachiosaurus*, but they measured only 20 feet (6.2 m) long, from snout to tail tip. *Brachiosaurus*, by comparison, grew up to 82 feet (25 m) long. By analyzing cross sections of these small sauropods' bones, scientists were able to determine that the animals were full-grown adults, not youngsters. Although the fossils were unearthed in Germany, fossils from the area surrounding the *Europasaurus* site were all of marine organisms, which led scientists to conclude that this sauropod fossil site was originally part of an offshore island, not part of the European mainland.

It is believed that insular dwarfs evolve as a response to the limited resources—especially food and water—typical of small oceanic islands. Smaller individuals are more likely to find sufficient resources to survive, grow, and reproduce than are larger individuals, which need larger quantities of these resources simply to survive. Over time, the larger individuals gradually die out and smaller ones take their place.

The South American sauropod *Amargasaurus* had neural spines that were longer than *Dicraeosaurus*. The plant-eating *Amargasaurus* was small for a sauropod, reaching a length of about 30 feet (10 m).

angled downward, placing the head near the ground. This, along with a low leg-length ratio, suggests that these dinosaurs were land-dwellers that frequented **riparian** habitats (areas bordering the edges of lakes and rivers), where they ate low-growing land plants and water plants growing near the shoreline.

This is in stark contrast to Mokele-mbembe, which reputedly spends most of its time in the water, not on the land bordering it, and feeds on vegetation that overhangs the water, sometimes at a considerable height. A dicraeosaurid body type does not seem suitable for such a lifestyle. The animal's low-slung head would be underwater a lot of the time, except in shallow water—a definite problem for an air-breather. With the additional complication of a low leg-length ratio, it might not be able to stretch its neck high enough to harvest the food it reputedly eats. In fact, those long neural spines might become entangled with each other if the neck were arched too high in the air.

One would expect an aquatic sauropod that fed on over-hanging vegetation to be built more like *Brachiosaurus*, with a high leg-length ratio and a neck capable of flexing to a near vertical position, producing a feeding envelope that readily encompassed the overhanging vegetation. The jury is still out, however, on the accuracy of the DinoMorph results. Some paleontologists suspect that sauropods' necks might have been more flexible than what DinoMorph predicts, in which case a dicraeosaurid just might be able to feed the same way Mokele-mbembe is supposed to.

The very suggestion that Mokele-mbembe is an aquatic sauropod is enough to convince many scientists that the creature is just a figment of the imagination. Many paleontologists are convinced that sauropods were the dinosaurian equivalent of the elephant, a terrestrial **megaherbivore** that only occasionally entered the water. Yet, the fact is, we just don't know whether there were any water-loving sauropods. According to American paleontologist Joanna Wright, "There are currently insufficient data . . . to make any general statements about sauropod habitat preferences. Sauropods were a globally distributed, long-lived group probably capable of exploiting a wide range of habitats . . . and climates." Anyway, the youngest dicraeosaurid fossils are more than 100 million years old. That's an incredibly long time; perhaps long enough for a terrestrial sauropod to evolve into an aquatic—or at least an **amphibious**—one.

Perhaps most sauropods were the terrestrial megaherbivores that most paleontologists envision. Some, however, may have spent a lot of time in the water. If all the strictly terrestrial specimens went extinct, while one small aquatic one *may* have survived to modern times, then maybe there was a crucial advantage to hanging out in the water. As we proceed, it will be important to try to find out what that advantage might be.

Reality Check

We've just taken a long, hard look at the creature known as Mokele-mbembe and tried to determine just what beast it might be. What has been suggested is pure speculation. That speculation, however, is based on sound scientific evidence. Hardened skeptics will claim that such conjecture is too far out to be taken seriously, while fans of Mokele-mbembe will be less critical, even supportive of what doubting Thomases might refer to as cryptozoological castles in the air. The bottom line is that unless and until someone obtains indisputable evidence that proves this beast exists, Mokele-mbembe will only reside in the realm of the imagination, not in the rain forest of the Congo Basin.

Lack of such evidence is not due to lack of effort. Many expeditions in search of Mokele-mbembe have been conducted over the past several decades. While no one has yet obtained that indisputable evidence, some adventurous investigators have come pretty close—or so they say. It's time for us to take a look at the most promising of these cases and see just how successful these dinosaur hunters have been.

THE SEARCH
BEGINS

Stories of the existence of large, dinosaurian creatures living in the central African rain forest go back
at least as far as the year the Declaration of Independence
was signed: 1776. In that year, a French missionary wrote
a book about the natural history of the Congo. Along with
descriptions of the plants and animals of the rain forest,
Abbe Lievain Bonaventure provided an account of his discovery of some huge footprints, 3 feet (1 m) in circumfer-
ence (about a foot in diameter). The prints were similar to
an elephant's, except that they had claw marks. This was an
important detail. Elephant footprints don't leave claw marks,
because elephants don't have claws. Sauropods, however, did
have claws, and many of their fossil footprint tracks clearly
show claw marks. Thus, some cryptozoologists regard Abbe

Bonaventure's account as one of the oldest pieces of evidence supporting the existence of dinosaurs in the Congo.

In the early 1900s, the big-game hunter Carl Hagenbeck reported hearing numerous comments from residents of the Congo region about a creature that was part elephant, part dragon. A few years later, a German surveyor in Cameroon, the Congo's next-door neighbor to the northwest, reported hearing stories about a nasty, long-necked, long-tailed, elephant-sized creature that inhabited the rain forest.

In 1920, the world-famous Smithsonian Institution mounted an expedition to the African rain forest in search of Mokele-mbembe. The trek was tragically cut short when the train carrying the dinosaur hunters derailed, flipped over, and crushed several of the expedition's members.

Over the next several decades, stories about the African dinosaur surfaced from time to time, but it wasn't until the 1970s and 1980s that Mokele-mbembe really captured the attention of the cryptozoological community. The man most responsible for Mokele-mbembe's surge in popularity was Roy Mackal. Mackal had made a name for himself in the 1960s and 1970s when he participated in several expeditions to Scotland in search of the Loch Ness Monster. Although he was never able to prove that Nessie existed, Mackal became convinced that a large cryptid of some sort inhabited the dark, spooky waters of the loch.

Mackal published his findings and speculations about Nessie's identity in a popular book, *The Monsters of Loch Ness: The First Complete Scientific Study and Its Startling Conclusions*. His interest in Mokele-mbembe would also lead to a book, the highlight of which would be the recounting of his two expeditions to the Congo in search of the elusive sauropod.

CASE #1: THE MACKAL EXPEDITIONS

At the end of the 1970s, Mackal's interest in Nessie seemed to wane as he became ever more intrigued by rumors about

Mokele-mbembe. Finally, he and **herpetologist** James Powell, a crocodile expert, decided to launch an expedition to the Congo and try to find out more about the secretive sauropod. During a trip to Gabon in 1979, Powell had encountered a Bantu folk healer who described a large jungle beast—the "N'yamala"—that had all the characteristics of a sauropod. When Powell showed the folk healer a bunch of animal pictures, including dinosaur pictures from a children's book, the man pointed to the picture of *Diplodocus* and claimed that that animal looked like N'yamala. Naturally, Powell's interest was piqued. Mackal was equally intrigued when he heard of Powell's experience. Convinced that a huge reptilian creature, possibly a dinosaur, might actually exist in the tropical African rain forest, Mackal and Powell eagerly booked tickets for a flight to the Congo.

The 1980 Expedition

Mackal and Powell arrived in Impfondo, a small city perched along the western shore of the Ubangi River, a mighty tributary of the even mightier Congo River, in January 1980. With the invaluable help of a pygmy guide, Marien Ikole, and Catholic missionary Gene Thomas, the two dinosaur hunters embarked on a month-long trek through the Likouala Swamp, which lay due west of Impfondo. Ikole had heard of Mokele-mbembe and said that it looked like the sauropod in one of the pictures in an illustrated animal book that Mackal and Powell brought along on the expedition.

Traveling from town to town, the two explorers talked to people and questioned them about Mokele-mbembe. Many local people provided stories about the big creature that inhabited rivers and lakes and killed or drove away all the elephants and hippos. Unfortunately, none of these stories was from an eyewitness source. They were all second- or third-hand accounts: Someone had heard from an uncle or a friend's brother about a Mokele-mbembe that had been

spotted hanging out in a cave along the bank of the so-
and-so river; or someone's grandfather had seen a Mokele-
mbembe feeding on the plants growing along the shore of
this or that lake. The problem with such stories is that the
more people they pass through, the more likely they are to
change, and the less likely they are to be accurate.

Finally, Mackal and Powell were introduced to a real
Mokele-mbembe eyewitness, a Bantu named Firman
Mosomele. As a young boy 45 years earlier, Mosomele had
a frightening encounter with the animal while alone on a
small boat on a river near the town of Epena. He described
the creature as having a small head atop a red-brown neck
that was about 6 feet (2 m) long. As he hurriedly paddled
away, he caught a glimpse of a portion of the animal's
brown back. Mosomele said that the sauropod in Mackal
and Powell's picture book looked similar to the Mokele-
mbembe he saw. Obviously, one must take a traumatic
45-year-old childhood memory with a grain of salt. Mackal
and Powell, however, were impressed with this, their first
actual eyewitness account of an encounter with Mokele-
mbembe.

A few days later, the two dinosaur hunters heard
another eyewitness account, this time from a man named
Nicolas Mondongo. Several years before, Mondongo had
seen a huge Mokele-mbembe standing in water only 3 feet
(1 m) deep, so he got a good view of the beast. Its neck
was as thick as a man's thigh and was red-brown in color.
The head was decorated with a cockscomblike crest, and
the length of the animal, from snout to tail tip, was about
33 feet (10 m).

Mackal and Powell heard several more eyewitness
reports of Mokele-mbembe sightings by the time their
expedition ended. While returning to the United States,
the exhausted adventurers discussed the results of their

Swamps are found throughout the Congo, typically near the Congo River or rivers that connect to it. When Mackal and colleagues explored the Likouala Swamp in 1980 and 1981, native guides were needed to help them navigate the difficult terrain.

fact-finding expedition and came to the conclusion that "although rare, the Mokele-mbembes do exist and that they correspond to no other living forms known to science."

Despite the fact that many people they interviewed identified Mokele-mbembe as the sauropod in the animal picture book, Mackal and Powell wisely refrained from claiming that the rare beast was in fact a living dinosaur. Such an outlandish claim would require far more supporting evidence than mere eyewitness accounts.

Mackal really wanted to find that evidence. The only way to do that was to mount another expedition to the Likouala Swamp. That's just what he did, the very next year.

The 1981 Expedition

Mackal's second expedition to the Likouala Swamp began in late October 1981. This trip coincided with the end of the rainy season, so the waters in the swamp and nearby rivers would be high enough to allow Mackal and his companions to travel by boat, a means of travel much preferred to hiking on foot. Natives of the Congo Basin carve their

The 1981 Mackal expedition traveled by pirogue (a boat carved from a tree trunk) as it explored rivers in the Likouala region. In this photograph, two pygmy fishermen travel in a pirogue similar to the one that would have been used by the Mackal expedition.

own boats, called **pirogues**, out of large rain forest tree trunks. Pirogues look like dugout canoes, and although their sides rise only a few inches above the surface of the water, they are very maneuverable by experienced Bantus and pygmies and are the preferred way to travel through the Likouala.

This expedition was bigger and a lot more sophisticated than the first one. Although Ikole and Thomas were there for round two, Powell stayed behind. In his place were three other scientists: cryptozoologist Richard Greenwell, geologist Justin Wilkinson, and a Congolese zoologist, Marcellin Agnagna. Also on board were a professional photographer, two additional pygmy guides, and two Congolese security officers.

The equipment brought along on this venture included radio equipment, a **sonar** unit, guns—in case of any too-close-for-comfort encounters with a nasty dinosaur—and camera gear. Hauling all of this through the swamp on foot would have made for difficult and very slow travel, so the two pirogues used on this excursion were more a necessity than a luxury.

At one point during the expedition, the adventurers had two encounters with . . . something. In the first instance, while scouting a shady riverbank, the searchers heard a loud "plopping" sound, which was followed by a nearly foot-high wave that washed over one of the pirogues. A half-hour search of the area came up empty, so the source of the wave was never determined. It was decided that, although it *could* have been Mokele-mbembe, it could also have been something as ordinary as a hippo, even though hippos were not known to inhabit this stretch of the river.

In the second encounter, while exploring a deep river with sonar, a 20-foot-long (6-m) object was detected 20 feet (6-m) below the surface. It stayed still for several minutes and then moved off and disappeared. Again, although the object *could* have been Mokele-mbembe, its behavior suggested a more ordinary explanation: A large Nile crocodile resting on the bottom and then swimming away.

On another occasion, Mackal and his team were taken by a hunter to a riverbank where the hunter had found a trail made by some large animal as it hauled itself out of the river and plowed its way into the shoreline vegetation. Now a year old, the trail still showed signs of foot-wide footprints on the leaf-covered ground. Measuring 6 feet (2 m) high and 3 feet (1 m) wide, the trail was the right size to have been made by a half-grown forest elephant. The hunter, however, emphatically claimed that elephants don't flatten the vegetation the way this animal did. If an elephant didn't make the trail, *maybe* Mokele-mbembe did.

By the time the expedition ended in early December, Mackal had collected more than 30 eyewitness accounts of sauropodlike creatures, some of which had a frill similar to a rooster's comb on the back of the head. These stories, combined with the mysterious wave, the sonar recording, and the river-edge trail and footprints, served to whet the imaginations of Mackal and his fellow dinosaur hunters, but they provided no solid evidence for the existence of Mokele-mbembe.

As he considered all the likely explanations for the phenomenon called Mokele-mbembe, Mackal realized that, as much as he might have wished, he still could not claim that the mysterious monster reptile with a bad attitude was in fact a sauropod dinosaur. He had no solid evidence whatsoever to bolster so bold a claim.

After he returned to the United States, Mackal put his thoughts and experiences on paper and penned another popular book, *A Living Dinosaur? In Search of Mokele-Mbembe.* After considering the pros and cons of all the possibilities—dinosaurs, giant lizards, and the like—he had to conclude, "The mystery beckons, but pending new information gleaned from future expeditions, our speculations must rest here."

LET'S GET TECHNICAL: DINOSAUR FOOTPRINTS

Paleontologists utilize all sorts of fossils when they study dinosaurs. For example, fossilized teeth and bones give a good idea what the animals looked like, how large they grew, what they ate, and sometimes even why or how they died. Fossil eggs and nests provide information about dinosaur reproductive behavior. One of the most interesting types of fossil, however, has no physical substance to it whatsoever: a footprint.

There is actually a branch of paleontology devoted exclusively to the study of fossil footprints: **ichnology** (from the Greek word *ichnos*, meaning "footprint"). Ichnologists glean all sorts of information about dinosaurs from their footprints. By studying variations in the distance between an individual dinosaur's footprints, its walking or running speed can be estimated. By studying large trackways left by several individuals, ichnologists have determined that some dinosaurs, including sauropods, traveled in herds. By identifying the different types of footprints present at a given trackway, it's possible to get an idea of which species lived together at a given time and place.

Probably the most famous of all footprint trackways is located along the Paluxy River in Texas. There, a series of tracks shows a drama unfolding: a hunting theropod apparently on the trail of one member of a group of sauropods. We will never know how this drama ended, but without those footprints, we would never know that this prehistoric incident ever occurred. Nothing this dramatic has been discovered in the land of Mokele-mbembe, but by carefully studying any large footprints one may find in the Congo Basin, it should be possible to determine whether they were left by an elephant or a hippo . . . or a dinosaur.

CASE #2: THE REGUSTERS EXPEDITION

Herman Regusters was an electrical engineer who was intensely interested in Mokele-mbembe. He had contacted Mackal when he heard of Mackal's first expedition to the Congo Basin. He had offered to help conduct a second expedition in search of the enigmatic creature. With his expertise in satellite tracking systems and ready access to all the tracking equipment that would be needed, he could plot the expedition's position and progress through the Likouala Swamp with pinpoint accuracy. Mackal liked what he heard and asked Regusters to join his 1981 expedition.

Unfortunately, as preparations for the expedition progressed, relations between Mackal and Regusters soured, and the two parted ways. Mackal went on with his expedition, and Regusters organized one of his own.

Like Mackal's, Regusters's expedition took place in late 1981. Regusters's venture began a month before Mackal's, but at one point both groups were in the Congo at the same time. Regusters, however, centered his expedition at Lake Tele, and since Mackal never visited that famed dinosaur watering hole, the two groups never crossed paths.

On October 28, as the Mackal expedition was just getting started, Regusters's group zeroed in on its quarry. At 5:30 that evening, the team noticed large "perturbations" on the otherwise glassy-smooth surface of the lake. The source of these waves escaped detection, but the very next morning, the creature itself was spotted. At a distance of about 1 mile (1.6 km), a dark "long necklike member" was spotted. It stayed in view for five minutes and then submerged.

One week later, Regusters and his wife, Kia, the expedition's medical officer, heard a strange noise while investigating the Lake Tele shoreline: "The cry can best be described as starting with a low windy roar, then increasing to a deep-throated trumpeting growl. Sounds of a large beast making

Mokele-mbembe supposedly kills hippos or drives them out of its territory. No hippos reside in or near Lake Tele.

[its way] through the bush were clearly distinguishable, as it moved away from us farther into the swamp."

On another occasion, four expedition members observed a large object moving through the water 0.6 miles (1 km) away. Because of the distance, the dark brown hump wasn't clearly visible, but the witnesses said the object was too large to be the back of a hippo, and it wasn't the right shape to be a crocodile.

On November 27, Kia Regusters glimpsed a 6.5-foot-long (2-m) snakelike head and neck poking up out of the water. It swayed back and forth once and then sank straight down, like a sinking submarine periscope.

Despite all of these encounters with the strange beast in Lake Tele, no convincing photographic evidence was obtained, although one of Regusters's photos supposedly showed part of the creature's head as it submerged into the lake. Regusters blamed this lack of success on a combination of bad timing (where's a camera when you need one?), malfunctioning equipment (the high humidity wreaked havoc on the cameras and batteries), and the human factor (trouble focusing cameras and composing pictures before the camera-shy animal moved away or submerged).

Nevertheless, Herman Regusters indicated that he believed his expedition encountered a sauropod dinosaur. He even boldly suggested which one it was: "The Congo Basin could well be a living museum for the sauropod species *Antarctosaurus*." Fossil remains of this sauropod, like those of *Amargasaurus*, have been discovered in Cretaceous rocks in Argentina. *Antarctosaurus* did not have the exceedingly long neural spines characteristic of dicraeosaurids; but then again, neither did the animal Regusters described.

As certain as Regusters was of the identity of the beast in Lake Tele, his expedition didn't garner much more than a cold shoulder from the cryptozoological community, partly because he lacked persuasive photographic or other evidence to back his story. Another reason might possibly be because he had had a falling out with Mackal, who was highly respected by many cryptozoologists. As the next case will show, however, another cryptid hunter soon made just as bold a claim about Mokele-mbembe as Regusters did. This time, people noticed.

THE SEARCH CONTINUES

A year and a half after Marcellin Agnagna accompanied Roy Mackal on the 1981 expedition to the Likouala Swamp, he was back in the jungle looking for Mokele-mbembe. This expedition was notable in that everyone on the seven-member team was Congolese. As an official of the Ministry of Water and Forests of the People's Republic of the Congo, Agnagna was in charge of the whole operation. He was bound and determined to find that dinosaur.

CASE #3: THE AGNAGNA EXPEDITION

Agnagna's adventure, which he described in detail in an article in *Cryptozoology* (the official journal of the International Society of Cryptozoology [ISC]), began in April 1983. The

Lake Tele is said to be one of Mokele-mbembe's favorite hideouts. Its dark, murky water makes it difficult for cryptid hunters to find anything underwater, including submerged sauropods. In this photo, a circle of clouds is reflected in the mirrorlike surface of the lake.

expedition team took a plane from Brazzaville, the capital of the People's Republic of the Congo, to Epena, located on the Likouala aux Herbes River in the Likouala Swamp. From there, the dinosaur hunters went by boat to the remote village of Boha, which is 37 miles (60 km) west of Lake Tele, Agnagna's final destination. The last leg of the journey was done on foot, as there was no easy river access to the lake. After two days of hiking through the swamp, the Congolese team arrived at the shore of the fabled lair of Mokele-mbembe.

Seek and Ye Shall Find

There was no sign of Mokele-mbembe for the first two days of Agnagna's stakeout at Lake Tele, although the team did catch several glimpses of an absolutely humongous turtle swimming in the lake. According to Agnagna, the turtle's shell was 6.5 feet (2 m) long. If so, this in itself was an amazing discovery, as that would have been the largest freshwater turtle ever seen by human eyes. This was definitely no ordinary lake.

LET'S GET TECHNICAL: LAKE TELE

Lake Tele lies 100 miles (160 km) north of the equator in the middle of the Likouala Swamp in the northeastern region of the People's Republic of the Congo. The lake is shaped like a slightly flattened circle, about 2 miles (3.2 km) in diameter. It is fed by several streams that drain water from the surrounding swamplands. This water contains a lot of decomposing plant and animal matter, and as a result, Lake Tele is very murky. In fact, visibility is often limited to the top several inches of water.

As all this **organic** material decomposes, large quantities of nutrients are released into the warm 85°F (29°C) water, creating a thriving community of plants and animals. More than 15 species of fish live there, along with turtles and countless crabs, shrimp, and clams.

Plants from the surrounding jungle grow right up to, and even overhang, the edge of the lake, where the water is only about 3 feet (1 m) deep. There is no beach; a large herbivore could easily stand in the water at lake's edge and munch away on all the tasty leaves and fruits growing there—which is exactly what the natives say Mokele-mbembe does.

On the third day, Agnagna found his dinosaur. During the early afternoon, he and two other members of the team set out to explore the nearby swamp. While Agnagna was busy filming a troop of monkeys in the trees above, one of his companions, Jean Dinkoumbou, slipped and fell in a mud puddle. Agnagna continued filming the monkeys with his movie camera while Dinkoumbou went to the lake to clean up.

A few minutes later, Dinkoumbou yelled to his companions to come quickly to the lake. Agnagna stopped filming and hurried over to join Dinkoumbou, who was standing by the shore and pointing to something far out on the lake. Peering through the thick vegetation at lake's edge, Agnagna glimpsed a large object on the lake's surface, some 980 feet (300 m) offshore.

To get a better look, Agnagna took the movie camera and waded about 200 feet (60 m) into the lake, filming the object the whole time. Then, as the film ran out (he had already used up most of it filming the monkeys), Agnagna realized that he had forgotten to remove the lens cap from the front of the camera. Nevertheless, he continued to view the object for 20 minutes through the movie camera's telephoto lens. What Agnagna saw was truly astounding: a tiny head perched atop a slender, 6-foot-long (2 m) neck, followed by the top portion of the animal's back, 10 feet (3 m) in length. The front of the neck was brown, but the rest of the animal was black. Agnagna included a drawing of the creature he saw in his report in *Cryptozoology*.

The creature eventually submerged, at which point the three excited men rushed back to camp, hopped in a pirogue, and returned to the spot of the sighting. They cruised the area for some time, video camera in hand, but the animal did not reappear. Nonetheless, Agnagna knew what he saw: "It can be said with certainty that the animal we saw was Mokele-mbembe, that it was quite alive, and, furthermore, that it is known to many inhabitants of the Likouala region. Its total length from head to back visible above the waterline was estimated at 5 meters [16 feet]." (While Agnagna was careful to avoid claiming in this report that his Mokele-mbembe was a sauropod dinosaur, he did make such a claim in separate correspondence with Mackal.)

An article published in the *ISC Newsletter* recounted Agnagna's adventure and provided additional details that seemed to **corroborate** Agnagna's story. In particular, the article stated that when Agnagna's ill-fated movie film was processed at a film-developing lab in France, "the end of the film developed black." That's exactly what would have been expected if the lens cap had been left on the lens while Agnagna was filming Mokele-mbembe.

Many eager cryptozoologists were thrilled with Agnagna's story. Some doubting Thomases, however, questioned some of the details, starting with, of all things, that silly little lens cap.

The Skeptics Speak Up

The next issue of *Cryptozoology* contained critical comments from a number of people who had read Agnagna's article. Also included were responses to those comments by Richard Greenwell, who served as the journal's editor, and by Agnagna himself. French paleontologist Pascal Tassy was quick to point out that the movie camera Agnagna claimed to have used when filming Mokele-mbembe and the monkeys, a Minolta XL-42, is a single lens reflex camera. In this type of camera, there is only one lens, which projects an image both onto the film and through the viewfinder. The viewfinder does not have its own lens. Therefore, if the lens cap was still on, anyone looking through the viewfinder would see exactly what the film saw: absolutely nothing—total blackness, which is just what the film supposedly recorded.

Agnagna should have noticed immediately that this was the case, not later, after the film ran out.

Tassy emphasized the grave significance of this seemingly minor inconsistency. "This particular wrong detail could cast doubt and unreliability on the entire report," he said, "and, by implication, could make the journal itself questionable."

Greenwell responded to this harsh criticism by taking full responsibility for the error. The mistake was a result of "a translation ambiguity [Agnagna's original manuscript was written in French, not English] and incorrect verbal information received from a third party in the Congo." As it turns out, the lens cap had been removed, but the lens was set for "macro," or close-up filming. (A macro lens is used for filming or photographing objects at very close range—like a bee on a flower. Any object in the far distance—like a monkey in a tree—would be thrown out of focus.) Once the mistake was publicized, a revised version of Agnagna's paper was published. In this new version, the statement, "the author unfortunately began filming with the lens cap on," was replaced with, "the author unfortunately began filming in the macro position."

Glen Kuban, an amateur paleontologist, took exception to Agnagna's assertion that what he saw on Lake Tele was Mokele-mbembe. Citing the great distance involved (a minimum of 790 feet [240 m]—the equivalent of more than two-and-a-half football fields) and the fact that the animal was mostly submerged and out in open water, making size estimation very difficult, Kuban thought Agnagna wasn't justified in claiming that what he saw was, without a doubt, Mokele-mbembe. Kuban thought Agnagna should have considered the possibility that what he saw was some other known animal: either another super-huge turtle or a big snake, such as a python.

In his response to Kuban, Agnagna claimed that what he saw could not have been a turtle because the neck was too large for the body. (This was a rather odd response, inasmuch as most of the body was submerged and therefore not clearly visible.) As for a big python, Agnagna correctly pointed out that a snake swimming out in the open would not be able to rear its head up out of the water the way this creature did. With no ground to support it, the snake's neck would simply slip back down into the water.

Finally, Christine Janis, the paleontologist previously quoted regarding the likelihood of sauropods living in the Congo Basin, commented on the possibility that the Agnagna expedition was a hoax. She did not claim that it *was*, only that it *might* be. She was right. For that matter, the same could be said for the Regusters expedition, because neither of these expeditions came back with sufficient evidence to back the bold claims of their leaders.

Up to this point, Mackal, Regusters, and Agnagna had all searched for Mokele-mbembe, and none of them (despite some confident claims to the contrary) had been able to prove that the animal exists. Serious cryptozoologists, however, are a persistent lot, and many others have followed in these dinosaur hunters' footsteps—and boat wakes—with the hope of finding that proof. So before we bring the search for the dinosaur to a close, we need to find out what, if anything, these other adventurers have discovered.

THE SEARCH CONTINUES

At least a half dozen dinosaur-hunting expeditions have been conducted in the Congo since Agnagna's 1983 venture. Some of the highlights follow.

Rory Nugent, 1985

In 1985, adventurer and journalist Rory Nugent trekked to Lake Tele to look for Mokele-mbembe. Nugent endured leeches "the size of a vacuum cleaner nozzle," ants in his pants—literally!—and pesky bees. He barely missed being smashed by a falling tree trunk during a violent nighttime thunderstorm, and was startled out of his wits by a roaring gorilla. Despite all these distractions, Nugent made his way to Lake Tele with the help of Bantu guides. Reflecting on his close encounter with the gorilla, Nugent couldn't help but wonder about the frightful noises and branch-shaking ruckus made by the big silverback he glimpsed through the dense vegetation: "Listening to its unearthly sounds, half-animal and half-human, I wonder how often a gorilla has been mistaken for Mokele-mbembe."

On his last day at Lake Tele, Nugent was rewarded with a sighting of . . . something. A bit more than a half mile (1 km) away, he saw a periscope-shaped object sticking up out of the water. As he jumped from the shore into a pirogue and started to paddle toward the periscope, he was stopped cold by his Bantu guides, who furiously aimed their spears and guns at him and ordered him to get out of the boat. Jumping back ashore, Nugent was scolded: "The god can approach man, but man never approaches the god. He would have killed us all."

Nugent never did find out what that periscope was. It's interesting to note, though, that elephants were heard trumpeting in the distance a short time before the periscope was sighted, and elephants sometimes swim in deep water with their trunk held up above the surface in order to breathe. The only evidence for Mokele-mbembe that Nugent was able to obtain was a couple of pictures, one showing a tiny, distant black blotch floating in the middle of the lake and the other an extremely out-of-focus and completely unidentifiable white-and-black blob floating on the water. Nugent wrote about his experience in his book *Drums along the Congo*.

Redmond O'Hanlon, 1989

Redmond O'Hanlon, another adventurous journalist, traveled to the Likouala Swamp in 1989. Battling malaria, adopting an orphaned baby gorilla, and marveling at the columns of notorious driver ants ransacking his hut, O'Hanlon was accompanied by Agnagna as he searched for the ever-elusive sauropod. At one point, O'Hanlon found himself wondering whether Agnagna's Mokele-mbembe might have been nothing more than an elephant walking on the bottom of Lake

Redmond O'Hanlon described his search for Mokele-mbembe in his book *No Mercy: A Journey into the Heart of the Congo*. Here, O'Hanlon is seen standing beside numerous dinosaur fossils.

Tele, "its trunk held curving up and forward as a breathing tube (Mokele-mbembe's neck) and only the hump of its back showing above the surface."

O'Hanlon never did find a sauropod—or swimming elephants, for that matter—in the lake. He recounted his adventures in his book *No Mercy: A Journey to the Heart of the Congo.*

CryptoSafari, 2001

In 2001, a joint expedition involving two cryptozoological organizations, CryptoSafari and the British Columbia Scientific Cryptozoology Club, traveled to Cameroon, the Congo's northwestern neighbor, to follow up on reports of Mokele-mbembe from this region of the Congo Basin. The expedition was assisted by several pygmy guides and porters, some of whom shared their own experiences of Mokele-mbembe with the expedition members. In one case, a pygmy who had been unable to haul his fishing net up from the river bottom ran away in terror when he decided that a Mokele-mbembe was sitting on his net. The expedition failed to find the sauropod.

More Dinosaurs?

Despite cryptozoologists' lack of success in finding dinosaurs in the African jungle, they keep looking. They're not just looking for sauropods. Unbelievable as it may seem, information collected by Mackal and others indicates that other types of dinosaur may also inhabit the Congo Basin— fantastic creatures with horns on their heads and bony plates sticking out of their backs. No wonder the search goes on!

SAUROPODS, CERATOPSIDS, AND STEGOSAURS

When they interview native Bantu and pygmy residents of the Congo, hunters of Mokele-mbembe sometimes hear bizarre descriptions of the creature. In fact, sometimes it seems as though totally different animals are being described. As it turns out, that may be the case. It appears that the name "Mokele-mbembe" means different things to different people. To some, it means the sauropod look-alike that we have been pursuing all along. But to others, the name means something less specific. Instead of referring to just one type of animal, it's applied collectively to several completely different mystery beasts that haunt the Likouala Swamp. In some cases, descriptions of the beasts seem to be a blend of traits of different creatures, which complicates an already confusing situation. The strangest part of all is that the descriptions of some of these other animals sound suspiciously like real dinosaurs, and some of them are clearly not of the sauropod variety.

DINOSAURS GALORE

One feature of Mokele-mbembe that is sometimes mentioned by eyewitnesses is a rather curious one: a large tooth or horn projecting from the animal's head. Some people claim that Mokele-mbembe uses this horn to attack elephants and hippos that trespass into its territory. No known sauropod is known to have sported such a structure. Other types of dinosaur did, though, and some Mokele-mbembe fans think that the little sauropod may not be the only dinosaur species hiding out in the Congo Basin.

Centrosaurus?

Among the last dinosaurs to flourish in the Mesozoic Era were the **ceratopsids**, or horned dinosaurs. This group reached its heyday toward the end of the Cretaceous Period, and was one of the last types of dinosaur to become extinct. The most famous of the ceratopsids was three-horned *Triceratops*, the species commonly portrayed in illustrations pitted against *T. rex* in a fight to the death: teeth and claws vs. horns and frill.

There were many species of ceratopsid, each characterized by a different shaped bony frill mounted on top of the skull and decorated with horns of varying size and number. Possibly the most bizarre-looking of all ceratopsids was *Styracosaurus*, which had six horns sticking out from the

One explanation for the horn some eyewitnesses see on Mokele-mbembe's head is that it actually belongs to another dinosaur, the one-horned ceratopsid *Centrosaurus*, which may also inhabit the Likouala region. This artist's model of *Centrosaurus* is located at a park in Canada.

edge of its frill, like spokes on a wheel, plus one large horn over its nose. The species we're concerned with, *Centrosaurus*, was more modestly decorated. *Centrosaurus* had a single large horn on the snout and a modest fanlike frill at the back of the skull. It was a dinosaurian version of a one-horned rhinoceros.

Residents of the Likouala region claim that a horned creature by the name of Emela-ntouka (which means "killer of elephants") lives in the swamp. From their description (bulky body, stout legs, massive tail, horned snout), this beast sounds remarkably similar to *Centrosaurus*. The only discrepancy is in the frill: Emela-ntouka doesn't have one. Still, some cryptozoologists believe that Emela-ntouka just might be a ceratopsid descendant of something similar to *Centrosaurus*. Others have suggested that the animal might be an unknown species of giant, water-loving rhinoceros, the discovery of which would be momentous in its own right.

Stegosaurus?

Our last unknown beast from the Likouala Swamp is perhaps the most outlandish of all. While staying in the village of Epena during his first expedition to the Congo, Roy Mackal was astounded when a woman looked through Mackal's picture book of prehistoric animals and pointed at one in particular, saying that her ancestors had talked about an animal like this one, the one "with the planks growing out of its back." She was pointing at a picture of *Stegosaurus*, the dinosaur with a double row of bony plates—"planks"?—sticking straight up along its back, along with four menacing spikes decorating the tip of its tail.

According to the woman, this creature, called Mbielu-mbielu-mbielu, frequented the water, and its planks were coated with water plants, like the film of **algae** that often grows on the shells of aquatic turtles. Mackal was flabbergasted at this woman's story. It was beginning to sound as though the Likouala Swamp housed a whole menagerie of dinosaurs!

Reality Check

OK, it's time for another reality check. Let's stop for a moment and take a dinosaur head count: *Amargasaurus, Dicraeosaurus, Centrosaurus, Stegosaurus*. That's four dinosaurs whose existence in modern times is being considered. Die-hard skeptics must be rolling their eyes by now:

"Sauropods, ceratopsids, and stegosaurs living together in an African swamp? You have to be kidding!" They have a point, at least as far as *Centrosaurus* is concerned. That's because no ceratopsid fossils have been found outside western North America. There's no evidence that these animals ever tread on African soil.

Now what about *Stegosaurus*? Again, its fossil remains have been found only in North America. However, a relative of *Stegosaurus* named *Kentrosaurus* did live in Africa. Its

One eyewitness in the Congo told cryptozoologist Roy Mackal that she knew of a beast with planks sticking up out of its back. Could it be a descendant of the African stegosaur *Kentrosaurus*? An artist's model of the prehistoric creature is pictured here.

fossil remains have been found in the same Tanzanian fossil site where *Dicraeosaurus* was discovered. So it's at least *possible* that some type of stegosaur inhabited the Congo Basin region at some point in the distant past and managed to survive to modern times.

Unfortunately, it's hard to come by fossils in the African rain forest. It's much easier to find them in arid lands, where overlying soil and rocks have been weathered away, exposing fossils that were buried millions of years ago. If someone had discovered sauropod, ceratopsid, and stegosaur fossils in the Congo, the survival of these dinosaurs into modern times would be a less preposterous idea. Those fossils, however, if they are there, remain buried beneath the rain forest floor, hidden from the searching eyes of paleontologists.

In order to make an educated guess on the likelihood of any dinosaurs surviving in the Likouala Swamp—or anywhere else, for that matter—one last factor needs to be considered: **extinction**. Just what catastrophic event at the end of the Cretaceous Period led to the demise of the dinosaurs? What factor common to a few lucky species might have enabled them to escape the fate suffered by all the others? Read on to consider these critical questions.

What Killed the Dinosaurs?

*C*ryptozoological investigations are not easy. Neither are paleontological investigations. That's not surprising, since both studies often seek information about the very same animals. The main difference is that paleontologists believe that these animals are extinct, whereas cryptozoologists believe that these animals still exist, despite the story the fossils tell. Mokele-mbembe is one famous example. Another is the Loch Ness Monster, which some cryptozoologists believe to be a plesiosaur, a huge marine reptile that presumably became extinct along with the dinosaurs at the end of the Cretaceous Period, 65 million years ago.

Just what happened 65 million years ago? Was there a sudden cataclysm of such tremendous magnitude that it single-handedly wiped out all the dinosaurs and marine reptiles in what, geologically speaking, was just a "blink of an eye"? Surely a disaster of such scope and intensity would have left behind more than enough evidence for scientists to figure out exactly what happened.

If only that were true.

EXTINCTION SCENARIO #1: ASTEROID IMPACT

There are actually several possible explanations for the **mass extinction** that wiped out so many species at the end of the Cretaceous. Some explanations rely on relatively gradual processes that lasted for millions of years (still a blink of the geological eye, since life has existed on Earth for a few *billion* years), slowly but surely killing off one dinosaur species after another, until none were left. One explanation, however, involves an event that was sudden indeed, wiping out the dinosaurs in a matter of weeks, months, or a few years at most. The event: a collision with an **asteroid**.

Kaboom!

In the 1970s, a group of geologists was studying layers of **sedimentary rock** on a mountain in central Italy, near the town of Gubbio. Led by the Nobel Prize-winning scientist Walter Alvarez, the team was investigating a 65 million-year-old rock layer dating back to the boundary between the Cretaceous and Tertiary Periods, the so-called K/T boundary. (The K stands for *Kreide*, the German term for Cretaceous; the T stands for Tertiary.)

While trying to determine how long it took for the K/T layer to be deposited, the group made an exciting, unexpected discovery. The K/T layer contained an unusually high concentration of the metallic element iridium. While iridium is extremely rare in rocks from the Earth's crust, it is much more common in certain types of meteorites that have crash-landed on Earth. Putting two and two together,

An asteroid that collided with Earth 65 million years ago, near what is now known as the town of Chicxulub on Mexico's Yucatan Peninsula, may have led to the extinction of the dinosaurs.

the scientists proposed that the high iridium content of the K/T layer was the result of an asteroid that crashed into our planet 65 million years ago. On impact, the asteroid would have exploded, sending a huge cloud of dust high into the air. This cloud, with its high iridium content, would have spread over the whole Earth before gradually settling back down on the surface, where it eventually formed part of the K/T rock layer analyzed by Alvarez 65 million years later.

The timing of this asteroid impact coincided nicely with the extinction of the dinosaurs, so the Alvarez team set the scientific world abuzz by proposing that the asteroid impact wiped out the dinosaurs.

According to the impact theory, the thick, dark dust cloud that blanketed Earth blocked out so much sunlight that plants died and temperatures fell to frigid levels. Even if sauropods and other herbivorous dinosaurs didn't succumb to the cold, they would have eventually starved to death. Carnivores such as *T. rex* would follow suit when their prey disappeared and they ran out of corpses to scavenge. Then, after the cloud settled and sunlight once again reached the Earth's surface, seeds sprouted, vegetation returned, and animals that survived the catastrophe, such as small mammals that hid in their cozy little burrows and managed to subsist on the little food available, repopulated the planet and ushered in the Age of Mammals.

The Evidence Mounts

In the years since the Alvarez team announced its asteroid impact theory, sedimentary K/T rocks in different locations throughout the world have been analyzed for their iridium content. They, too, have been shown to have an unusually high concentration of this rare element. Then, with the 1990 discovery of a 65 million-year-old impact crater near the small town of Chicxulub, on the tip of Mexico's Yucatan Peninsula, it seemed that the "smoking gun" responsible for the extinction of the dinosaurs had been found.

Things, however, are often not as simple as they first appear. Such was the case with the Alvarez theory. Certain details in the fossil record suggested that the asteroid impact told only part of the story behind the extinction of the dinosaurs. It would appear that the asteroid had an accomplice or two . . . or three.

EXTINCTION SCENARIO #2: VOLCANIC ERUPTIONS

As it turns out, close study of the fossil record from the end of the Cretaceous Period indicates that the dinosaurs didn't all die out at the exact same instant. Some types had already become rare by the time the asteroid struck, which suggests that they were already on the road to extinction. Also, a few dinosaur fossils have been found in North American Tertiary sediments deposited after the asteroid impact, which suggests that some dinosaurs actually survived the impact. Perhaps some dinosaur eggs survived the impact and hatched after the dust cloud settled, enabling a few species to recover—temporarily.

What this means is that something else was probably going on prior to and possibly after the asteroid impact, slowly pushing the dinosaurs toward extinction. The asteroid may just have been the final blow that wiped out most of what was left of a group of animals already on its way to oblivion.

The Deccan Traps

At the end of the Cretaceous Period, India was a huge island located in what is now the Indian Ocean. Riding northward on the Australian tectonic plate, India was still millions of years and thousands of miles away from its collision with the Asian plate, which would result in the formation of the Himalaya mountains. All, however, was not quiet on the migrating island. From 69 million to 63 million years ago, India was plagued with on-again, off-again volcanic activity that produced huge lava flows. This lava ultimately covered 770,000 square miles (1,970,000 square km) of west-central India with a thick blanket that hardened into **basalt** rock, in some places up to 8,000 feet (2,440 m) thick! This basalt blanket is known as the Deccan Traps.

Along with all that lava, the volcanoes of the Deccan Traps spewed carbon dioxide (CO_2) and **particulates** (microscopic bits and pieces of solid material) into the atmosphere, creating one nasty case of worldwide air pollution. Many scientists believe that the increase in CO_2, a **greenhouse gas**, may have caused significant **global warming**. Other scientists believe that particulate matter spewed into the atmosphere may have formed clouds that blocked sunlight and produced cooling instead of warming. In either case, Earth's climate would have changed significantly at the end of the Cretaceous Period, and dinosaurs may have found it difficult to cope.

EXTINCTION SCENARIO #3: MARINE REGRESSION

Another factor that may have contributed to the demise of the dinosaurs is a phenomenon called **marine regression**, a gradual drop in sea level. During the early Cretaceous Period, the Earth was so warm that there were no polar ice caps. As a result, sea level was much higher than it is today, and much land that now lies above sea level was then at the bottom of shallow seas. The best known of these inland Cretaceous seas is the Western Interior Sea, which cut through the middle of the North American continent, extending from the state of Texas all the way up to Montana and North Dakota and on into Canada. This inland sea averaged only a few hundred feet deep and, baked under the hot Cretaceous sun, was a very warm and productive sea that teemed with aquatic life. Everything from fish and clams to plesiosaurs and other marine reptiles thrived there.

Starting during the Jurassic Period and continuing through the Cretaceous Period, something happened. An ancient tectonic plate, the Farallon plate, subducted beneath the western edge of the North American plate. This

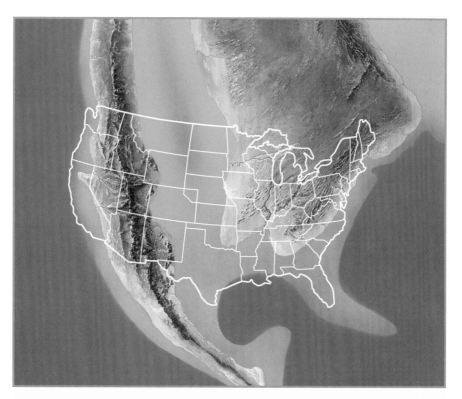

Regression of the shallow, productive Western Interior Sea during the Cretaceous Period eliminated choice coastal dinosaur habitats and may have contributed to the extinction of the dinosaurs.

subduction process created the Rocky Mountains and gradually elevated the Midwestern states above sea level. The result was as if someone had pulled the plug on a giant bathtub, allowing the water of the inland sea to slowly drain away. As the Western Interior Sea receded, aquatic and shoreline habitats slowly disappeared, and animals that depended on these habitats gradually followed suit. The overall result was a reduction in the number of animal species, including dinosaurs, surviving by the end of the Cretaceous Period.

Regression of inland seas happened on other continents as well, and probably contributed in a big way to a worldwide reduction in the number of animal species, including dinosaurs.

EXTINCTION SCENARIO #4: INSECTS

The three extinction scenarios considered so far have **abiotic**, or nonliving, causes: an asteroid, volcanoes, and shrinking seas. The next scenario involves **biotic**, or living, factors. You might think that a biotic factor that would cause the extinction of animals as big and powerful as dinosaurs would itself be big and powerful. In fact, the reverse may be true. What may have contributed to the extinction of the dinosaurs could have been as small and delicate as a tiny insect.

Insects? The mighty dinosaurs might have been wiped out by mere insects? That's right. Insects have been around for hundreds of millions of years, and they thrived in the heat of the Cretaceous Period. No one is suggesting that a single species of insect caused the extinction of the dinosaurs. Rather, innumerable species, each in its own way, may have contributed to the dinosaurs' demise.

Insects as Competitors

Anyone who has planted a vegetable garden knows that herbivorous insects are a real nuisance. They can wreak havoc on row after row of lettuce, beans, corn, celery—you name it and there's a host of insects just waiting to munch away on it. It is quite possible that forests and fields of the Cretaceous Period were beset by plagues of insects every bit as destructive as modern-day plagues of locusts that lay to waste entire fields of agricultural crops. If super-plagues of insects munched their way through enough vegetation, whole herds of herbivorous dinosaurs could have gone hungry and possibly starved to death.

There is evidence that such insects lived during the Cretaceous Period. Herbivorous leafhoppers and locustlike grasshoppers (all very similar in appearance to their modern crop-devastating descendants) sometimes got stuck in sticky tree sap and turned into fossils as the sap slowly hardened and turned into a rock-hard substance called **amber**. Amber is a clear, brownish substance that preserves the remains of any insect unlucky enough to become mired in the sap. These remains are so well preserved that even the tiniest, most delicate body part can be observed in its original state.

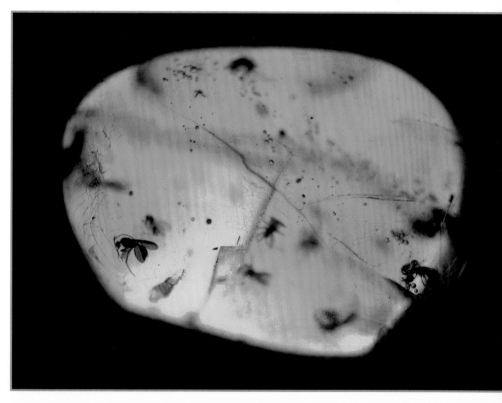

These insects from prehistoric times became mired in tree sap. The sap hardened over time and turned into rock-hard amber, preserving the insects in great detail.

Only a tiny percentage of Cretaceous insects became fossilized in amber, and only a tiny percentage of these has been collected by paleontologists. Therefore, one can only conclude that insect species that paleontologists have found in amber must have existed in huge numbers—possibly huge enough to form swarms that devastated the local flora as they moved from one feast to another, leaving a lot of hungry dinosaurs in their wake.

Insects as Vectors of Plant Disease

As if that wasn't enough, some insects may have wiped out whole populations of certain plant species, not by eating them, but by spreading deadly plant diseases—particularly plant-infesting **fungi**—from sick plants to healthy ones. Such diseases could eventually kill the biggest tree, even if the insect **vector** that spread the disease didn't eat a single leaf.

The devastating effect of such insect-transmitted plant diseases was witnessed in action in the 1900s, when chestnut blight, a fungus spread by bark beetles, killed 99% of all specimens of the majestic American chestnut tree—several *billion* trees in all—in just 50 years. These beetles eat the fungus, and when they lay eggs under the bark of healthy trees, they contaminate the healthy wood with the deadly fungus to provide food for the grubs when they hatch. With millions of these beetles hop-scotching their way from tree to tree, the fungal disease spread like wildfire across the whole Eastern United States. Bark beetles have been found in Cretaceous amber, so it is possible that these insects were as destructive back then as they have been in modern times.

Insects as Vectors of Dinosaur Disease

Insects are vectors of animal disease, too. In fact, some of the worst diseases afflicting mankind are spread by flies and mosquitoes, including one of the most widespread and deadly diseases of all: malaria. This horrible affliction, caused by a microscopic, single-celled **protozoan**, is spread from victim to victim by certain biting flies and mosquitoes. Symptoms

LET'S GET TECHNICAL: MALARIA

The life cycle of the malaria parasite is a complicated one. The parasite begins its life cycle in the gut of a suitable species of biting, blood-feeding fly or mosquito. (Many parasites are **host-specific**: Different stages in the parasite's life cycle can only survive in certain species of host. If they are ingested by the wrong species of fly or mosquito, they will die.) The parasite begins life as one of many tiny, round **sporozoites**, which are encased in a protective **oocyst** that is attached to the inner wall of the fly's digestive tract. When mature, the now wormlike sporozoites hatch from the oocyst and make their way to the fly's **salivary glands**.

When the insect bites its vertebrate prey for a blood meal, its sporozoite-contaminated saliva enters the wound, and the sporozoites enter their vertebrate host. The sporozoites invade the liver of their new host and develop into **merozoites**. Mature merozoites then enter blood cells, where they develop into **gametocytes**.

When another fly bites the vertebrate host, it ingests gametocytes along with its blood meal. The gametocytes reproduce in the fly's gut, producing **ookinetes**, which attach to the gut wall, develop into oocysts, and start the life cycle anew.

All suitable biting flies and mosquitoes that take a blood meal from a single infected vertebrate can become infected with gametocytes and become vectors, spreading malaria far and wide, sickening whole populations of the vertebrate host. It has been suggested that protozoan parasites such as malaria may have played a significant role in the extinction of the dinosaurs.

of this disease include fever, shivers, sweating, and anemia. In severe cases, it can be fatal; in fact, one million people die from malaria every year.

Malaria is only one of scores of insect-borne protozoan diseases known to afflict vertebrates. At least a few of these protozoans, including malaria, are known to have existed during the Cretaceous Period. They, along with their fly vectors, have been discovered in amber dating back to that geologic period.

Amber fossil experts George and Roberta Poinar are convinced that insects played a role in the extinction of the dinosaurs. In their book *What Bugged the Dinosaurs?*, they

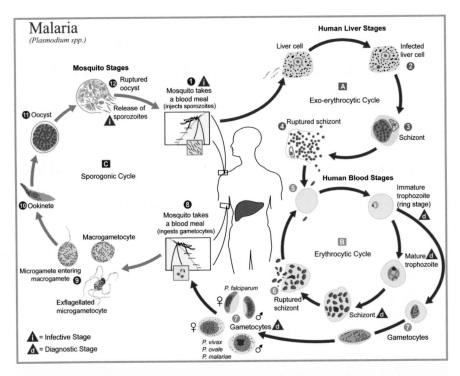

The malaria parasite has a very complicated life cycle that requires two separate hosts: an insect (a certain species of fly or mosquito) and a vertebrate, such as a human ... or a dinosaur.

picture swarms of disease-spreading insects descending on hapless dinosaurs having virtually no defense against all those tiny jaws gouging them and jabbing them and feeding off their blood. They write: "Most Cretaceous dinosaurs would have been fair game, especially the large, slow-moving sauropods that had no real protection against biting flies." There was probably only one escape from their assailants: "Some relief may have been found in water, and perhaps the large sauropods . . . submerged their under parts as much as possible for protection from the voracious biters."

Bingo! The deciding factor that might have enabled Mokele-mbembe to escape extinction could have been its aquatic lifestyle. Maybe living in water afforded the little sauropod just enough protection from insect-borne diseases that it managed to escape the fate suffered by all the other dinosaurs—except for, perhaps, Mbielu-mbielu-mbielu and Emela-ntouka, both of which, coincidentally, also like to hang out in the water.

All of which brings us to another important question: Could insect-born diseases such as malaria have wiped out the dinosaurs? Malaria, in particular, was a new disease in the Cretaceous Period. Perhaps dinosaurs hadn't had a chance to develop resistance to this disease before it started spreading like wildfire. Whole populations of dinosaurs could have been decimated by swiftly spreading **pandemics** that left few if any survivors.

Such scenarios have unfolded in our lifetimes. When West Nile virus, which is transmitted by mosquitoes, arrived in New York City in 1999 (it somehow hitchhiked its way from Israel to North America), it quickly spread westward. Within just a few years, millions upon millions of birds succumbed to a disease against which they had no resistance. Perhaps outbreaks of dinosaur malaria had similar dire consequences.

The idea that insect-borne diseases alone could have killed off the dinosaurs is doubtful. What seems most likely is that a combination of biotic and abiotic factors worked in concert to create an overwhelming challenge that even *T. rex* couldn't surmount.

EXTINCTION SCENARIO #5: THE QUADRUPLE WHAMMY

The fossil evidence indicates that the dinosaurs died out over at least several hundred thousand years, perhaps even a few million years. So it makes sense that their disappearance was affected by gradual, not sudden, forces that slowly took their toll, generation by generation, population by population, species by species.

Perhaps the decline of the dinosaurs began when marine regression began to wipe out a lot of prime dinosaur habitat along the shores of shrinking inland seas. Then, to add insult to injury, the climate deteriorated when volcanic eruptions of the Deccan Traps commenced. Then, right at the K/T boundary, an asteroid slammed into the Yucatan Peninsula, instantaneously wiping out huge numbers of dinosaurs that were still struggling along. Finally, facing severe climate changes wrought by these abiotic factors, the few dinosaurs that remained were no longer able to compete against the ever-present insects: Falling victim to the hordes of herbivorous bugs and disease-spreading insect vectors, the mighty reptiles became fewer and fewer and finally were gone.

Except, perhaps, for a small species of water-loving sauropod (and perhaps a stegosaur and a ceratopsid as well) that managed to beat the odds and survive to the present in a swamp in the middle of the Congo Basin.

FINAL REPORT ON MOKELE-MBEMBE

$\mathcal{M}$okele-mbembe is undoubtedly one of the most complicated of all cryptids. Not only do descriptions of this denizen of the Congo Basin vary from witness to witness, but a supernatural aura seems to surround this beast. According to the animist culture common to central Africa, the spirit of Mokele-mbembe is revered as a powerful rain forest god. Therefore, stories about the creature might be expected to be exaggerated or distorted to reflect this godlike status. Nevertheless, we have managed to gather a considerable body of information about this animal and are now in a position to summarize our findings.

SEARCHING FOR A LIVING SAUROPOD

When all descriptions of Mokele-mbembe are considered, one type of animal fits the bill better than any other: a long-necked, long-tailed, small-headed, bulky-bodied sauropod dinosaur. Many adventurous cryptid hunters have launched expeditions in search of this beast, hoping to be the first to lay eyes on a living dinosaur. In Case #1, we took a look at back-to-back expeditions by cryptozoologist Roy Mackal in 1980 and 1981. Surveying the Likouala Swamp in the northeastern People's Republic of the Congo, Mackal and his colleagues searched a wide area and collected eyewitness accounts of dozens of Mokele-mbembe sightings from the local Bantus and pygmies. Neither expedition, however, obtained incontrovertible evidence that the creature exists.

Similarly, expeditions led by Herman Regusters in 1981 (Case #2) and Marcellin Agnagna in 1983 (Case #3) failed to obtain concrete evidence that Mokele-mbembe exists, even though both men confidently claimed that the sauropod is alive and well and living in Lake Tele.

SPECULATIONS ON A LIVING SAUROPOD

We looked at what evidence there was, compared that evidence to what is known about sauropod dinosaurs, and nominated two genera as candidates for the title of "most likely ancestor of Mokele-mbembe": *Amargasaurus* and *Dicraeosaurus*. Each of these species may have possessed some sort of crest on the back of the head and neck—an extremely rare feature in sauropods, but one of the features commonly (but not invariably) described by Mokele-mbembe witnesses.

The investigation then took a look at dinosaur extinction in order to try to find out how one sauropod (and perhaps a stegosaur and a ceratopsid as well) could have beat the odds and survived the mass extinction that brought the Age of the Dinosaurs to an end. Marine regression of inland seas and volcanic activity in India probably contributed to the demise of countless dinosaurs before and after a death-dealing asteroid smashed into the Yucatan Peninsula 65 million years ago. Finally, the relentless onslaught of herbivorous and disease-spreading insects may have gradually finished off the limited numbers of dinosaurs that managed to survive the asteroid impact.

The key to Mokele-mbembe's ancestors' survival (and Emela-ntouka's and Mbielu-mbielu-mbielu's as well) might have been their aquatic nature: Unlike other, primarily terrestrial dinosaurs, they may have spent most of their time in the water, where they would have escaped the brunt of the onslaught of insect vectors infected with malaria and other deadly diseases. An aquatic sauropod would go against the conventional paleontological wisdom, which posits that sauropods were terrestrial megavertebrates that rarely hung out in the water. This decidedly unconventional aquatic lifestyle just might be what saved Mokele-mbembe's ancestors from extinction.

Enough with all this speculation. The plain and simple fact of the matter is that no one has produced convincing evidence showing that dinosaurs live in the Congo Basin (or anywhere else, for that matter). Still, as the old cryptozoological motto goes, absence of proof is not proof of absence. If Mokele-mbembe were discovered to be the real deal, it wouldn't be the first time an animal thought extinct for millions of years turned up alive and well, turning the scientific community on its head.

THE GLASS SPONGE REEF: A LIVING FOSSIL

The most famous example of the discovery of an "extinct" animal from the distant past occurred in 1938, when a live

The coelacanth was thought to have been extinct for 80 million years, until a live specimen was discovered in 1938.

coelacanth, a type of fish whose fossil record ended some 80 million years ago, was captured in the Indian Ocean along the east coast of Africa. The discovery of an even more unexpected "living fossil," however, occurred only two decades ago.

In 1987, scientists photographed an amazing sight in deep water off the west coast of British Columbia, Canada. Investigating sonar readings that showed a mysterious mound on the otherwise totally flat sea floor, the scientists obtained underwater photographs of the mound and discovered that they were looking at a huge reef. Not a coral reef, like Australia's famous Great Barrier Reef, but a reef of sponges—glass sponges, to be precise.

The fossil record indicated that reef-building glass sponges (relatives of the common bath sponge) became

Prior to the discovery of a living deep-water glass sponge reef off the coast of British Columbia, Canada, in 1987, reef-building sponges were thought to have been extinct for 100 million years.

extinct 100 million years ago. Yet, here they were, thriving at the bottom of the Pacific Ocean! When they saw the photos of the sponge reef, the scientists were flabbergasted. "When I first heard about the sponge reefs, I was electrified. It was like finding a living dinosaur," commented Paleontologist Manfred Krautter, who studies **invertebrates**. Marine biologist Verena Tunnicliffe explained how the glass sponge reef had managed to avoid discovery for so long: "What we know of these animals has been constrained by limited access to their habitat. That's why we didn't find them for so long."

The Mokele-mbembe situation is similar to the glass sponge reef situation. There is limited, or at least very difficult, access to much of the Congo Basin, especially the Likouala

Does an aquatic sauropod inhabit the lakes and rivers of the Likouala Swamp? Cryptozoologists continue to explore the area, hoping that the answer to this question is, "Yes!"

Swamp. Anyone who succeeds in finding Mokele-mbembe would surely be as electrified as Krautter was. It would be an amazing discovery indeed.

Skeptics think the search for a living dinosaur is an exercise in futility. Dedicated cryptozoologists beg to differ. What do you think?

GLOSSARY

Abiotic   Not living; not made by a living thing

Algae   Aquatic plants that lack stems, roots, and leaves; "seaweed"

Amber   Fossilized tree sap

Amphibious   Capable of living both on land and in water

Anatomy   The structure of an organism

Animism   The belief that every object in the natural world (for example, trees, animals, rivers, stones) has a soul

Archosaur   A group of reptiles that appeared more than 200 million years ago; the group includes pterodactyls (extinct flying reptiles), crocodiles, birds, and dinosaurs

Asteroid   A rocky object that orbits the Sun; most asteroids are found between the orbits of the planets Mars and Jupiter

Asthenosphere   The molten lower layer of Earth just below the lithosphere

Bantu   A group of people native to central and southern Africa; also, the language spoken by these people

Basalt   A type of rock made of solidified lava produced by erupting volcanoes

Biotic   Living or made by a living thing

Bipedal   Having two feet; humans and birds are bipedal

Ceratopsid   A horned dinosaur; characterized by a bony frill, often adorned with one or more horns; for example, *Centrosaurus* and *Triceratops*

Convergent boundary   The boundary between two converging (colliding) tectonic plates

Core   The centermost layer of Earth

Corroborate   To confirm or support

Cretaceous Period   The portion of the geologic time scale extending from approximately 145 million to 65 million years ago

Cryptid   A "hidden animal" that some people believe exists, even though there is insufficient evidence to prove its existence

Cryptozoology   The study of unknown or "hidden" animals

Crust   The outermost layer of Earth; Earth's surface

Cycad   A large tropical plant that possesses a clump of fernlike leaves sprouting from the top of a thick trunk

Dicraeosauridae   A group of sauropod dinosaurs characterized by extremely long neural spines projecting upward from the vertebrae

Dinosaur   An ancient group of reptiles that evolved from archosaurs and lived during the Mesozoic Era; examples include *T. rex* and *Brachiosaurus*

Divergent boundary   The boundary between two diverging (separating) tectonic plates

Extinction   The act of becoming extinct or dying out

Feeding envelope   The area within reach of the mouth of a feeding quadruped as it sweeps its neck up, down, and side-to-side

Femur   The upper leg bone

Fetish   An object (e.g., a pebble, tooth, or piece of hair) that is reported to possess a soul and may have supernatural power

Folk healer   A person who has been trained in divining (communicating with spirits) and the use of natural medicines; a "witch doctor"

Fungus (plural: fungi)   A plantlike organism that derives nourishment from dead or living organisms (e.g., a mushroom); some fungi produce disease by attacking living plants or animals

Gametocyte   One of the stages in the life cycle of the malaria parasite; specifically, the stage that reproduces, giving rise to the ookinete stage

Gastrolith   A stone found in the muscular gizzard of birds and dinosaurs, used to pulverize food; also called a "gizzard stone"

Genus (plural: genera)   One of the levels of taxonomic classification of organisms; it is composed of closely related species

Gizzard   A muscular organ of the digestive system that pulverizes or "chews" food; the gizzard may contain gastroliths that aid this process

Global warming   Warming of Earth's climate as a result of a buildup of greenhouse gases (especially carbon dioxide) that trap heat radiating from the planet's surface

Gondwana   A supercontinent—composed of Africa, South America, India, Australia, and Antarctica—which existed in the Mesozoic Era

Greenhouse gas   Any atmospheric gas (such as carbon dioxide) that traps heat near Earth's surface

Herbivore   A plant-eating animal

Herbivorous   Feeding mainly on plants

Herpetologist   A scientist who studies reptiles and amphibians

Host   An organism in or on which another organism lives

Ichnology   The study of fossil footprints

Immortal   Living forever, never dying

Insular dwarfism   A condition in which animals living on an island evolve (over many generations) a smaller body size in order to survive on the island's limited resources

Inundation   A flood

Invertebrate   An animal without a backbone; for example, insects and worms

Latitudinal position   A reference to a geographic location relative to the equator; measured in degrees ($0°–90°$) north or south of the equator

Lithosphere   The rigid outer layer of Earth, consisting of the upper mantle and crust

Lowland rain forest   Rain forest at an elevation less than 4,000 feet (1,200 m)

Mammoth   An extinct mammal related to modern-day elephants

Mantle   The layer of Earth that lies beneath the crust

Marine regression   A lowering of sea level

Mass extinction   An extinction event in which a huge percentage (at least 50%) of all species become extinct within a relatively short period of time; for example, the mass extinction at the end of the Cretaceous Period wiped out almost all of the dinosaurs

Megaherbivore   A very large plant-eating animal

Merozoite   One of the stages in the life cycle of the malaria parasite; specifically, the stage that develops into gametocytes

Mesozoic Era   The portion of Earth's history extending from 245 million to 65 million years ago

Montane rain forest   A rain forest at an elevation greater than 4,000 feet (1,200 m)

Neural spine   A bony projection sticking out from the top of a vertebra

Oocyst   A protective covering that shelters the sporozoite stage in the life cycle of the malaria parasite

Ookinete   The structure that gives rise to the oocyst of the malaria parasite

Organic   Of or made by living or once-living organisms

Ornithischian   A "bird-hipped" dinosaur whose hip bones appear similar to those of a bird

Paleontologist   A scientist who studies fossils

Pandemic   A widespread disease

Particulates   Very small bits of dust, soot, etc.

Pelvis   The hips

Pirogue   A boat similar to a dugout canoe, made from a carved-out tree trunk

Plate tectonics   The theory that proposes that Earth's surface is composed of several plates that move around and interact with each other, creating mountains, volcanoes, earthquakes, and the crust itself

Plesiosaur   A type of huge, long-necked marine reptile that lived at the time of the dinosaurs

Protozoan   A single-celled, animal-like organism; many protozoans are parasites that cause diseases (for example, malaria) in other organisms

Pterodactyl   A flying reptile that lived at the time of the dinosaurs

Pygmy   A group of people from the equatorial region of Africa, notable for their short stature (usually less than 5 feet [1.5 m]) tall

Quadrupedal   Having four feet; dogs are quadrupedal

Refuge   A sheltered or protected area

Relict   Surviving from an earlier time

Riparian   Of or referring to the banks of a river or lake

Salivary gland   A gland that secretes saliva into the mouth

Saurischian   A "lizard-hipped" dinosaur whose hip bones appeared similar to those of a lizard

Sauropod   A type of dinosaur characterized by a long tail, long neck, small head, large body, and pillarlike legs; examples include *Brachiosaurus* and *Diplodocus*

Seafloor spreading   The widening of the ocean floor as a result of the separation of tectonic plates sharing a divergent boundary

Sedimentary rock   A rock formed by the settling and compacting of soil particles, stones, mud, and silt on the bottom of rivers, lakes, and oceans

Sexual dimorphism   The condition in which males and females of an animal species have different characteristics, such as body size, presence or absence of antlers or crests, etc.

Skeptic   A person who relies on facts and reason, rather than wishful thinking or gut feelings, to draw a conclusion

Sonar (acronym for *sound navigation and ranging*)   A device that uses sound waves to detect underwater objects and surfaces

Sporozoite   The stage of the malaria parasite that hatches from an oocyst and makes its way to the salivary glands of its insect host

Subduction   The process in which one tectonic plate dives underneath another plate at a convergent boundary

Taxonomic   Of or pertaining to taxonomy, the branch of science that deals with the classification of organisms

Taxonomist   A scientist who classifies organisms

Theropod   A carnivorous, bipedal saurischian dinosaur; for example, *T. rex*

Transform boundary   The boundary between two tectonic plates that are sliding past each other

Vector   An animal (often an insect) that spreads disease to humans or other animals

Vertebra (plural: vertebrae)   One of the individual bones of the neck or backbone; an animal with a backbone is called a vertebrate

BIBLIOGRAPHY

BOOKS AND ARTICLES

Agnagna, Marcellin. "Neither Turtle nor Snake." *Cryptozoology* 3 (1984): 140–141.

———. "Results of the First Congolese Mokele-mbembe Expedition." *Cryptozoology* 2 (1983): 103–112.

Bakker, Robert T. *The Dinosaur Heresies: New Theories Unlocking the Mystery of the Dinosaurs and Their Extinction*. New York: William Morrow, 1986.

Collins, Mark, ed. *The Last Rainforests: A World Conservation Atlas*. New York: Oxford University Press, 1990.

"Congolese Biologist Observes Mokele-mbembe." *ISC Newsletter*. 2 (1983): 1–4.

Curry Rogers, Kristina A., and J.A. Wilson. *The Sauropods: Evolution and Paleobiology*. Berkeley: University of California Press, 2005.

Dybas, Cheryl Lyn. "Deep Sea Lost and Found." *Bioscience* 58 (2008): 288–294.

Emmer, Rick. *Virus Hunter*. Philadelphia: Chelsea House, 2006.

Everhart, Michael J. *Oceans of Kansas: A Natural History of the Western Interior Sea*. Bloomington: Indiana University Press, 2005.

Greenwell, Richard. "Response by the Editor." *Cryptozoology* 3 (1984): 137.

Janis, Christine M. "The Sauropod Hypothesis: An Evaluation of the Congolese Report on Mokele-mbembe." *Cryptozoology* 3 (1984): 141–144.

Kerr, Richard A. "Geoscience: From Earth's Core to African Oil." *Science*. 294 (2001): 287.

Kissel, Richard A. "The Sauropod Chronicles." *Natural History* 116 (2007): 34–38.

Kuban, Glen J. "Mokele-mbembe or Turtle?" *Cryptozoology* 3 (1984): 137–140.

Mackal, Roy P. *A Living Dinosaur: In Search of Mokele-Mbembe.* Leiden, Netherlands: E.J. Brill, 1987.

———. *The Monsters of Loch Ness: The First Complete Scientific Study and its Startling Conclusions.* Chicago: Swallow Press, 1976.

Martin, Claude. *The Rainforests of West Africa: Ecology, Threats, Conservation.* Basel, Switzerland: Birkhäuser Verlag, 1991.

Nugent, Rory. *Drums Along the Congo.* Boston: Houghton Mifflin, 1993.

O'Hanlon, Redmond. *No Mercy: A Journey to the Heart of the Congo.* New York: Alfred A. Knopf, 1997.

Paul, Gregory S., ed. *Book of Dinosaurs: The Best Minds in Paleontology Create a Portrait of the Prehistoric Era.* New York: Byron Press, 2000.

Poinar, George Jr., and R. Poinar. *What Bugged the Dinosaurs: Insects, Disease and Death in the Cretaceous Period.* Princeton, NJ: Princeton University Press, 2008.

Regusters, Herman A. *Mokele-Mbembe: An Investigation into Rumors Concerning a Strange Animal in the Republic of the Congo.* Pasadena: California Institute of Technology, 1982.

Salgado, Leonardo, and J.F. Bonaparte. "A New Dicraeosaurid Sauropod, *Amargasaurus cazaui* gen. et sp. nov., from the La Amarga Formation, Neocomian of Neuquén Province, Argentina." *Ameghiniana* 28 (1991): 333–346.

Strahler, Arthur N. *Science and Earth History.* Amherst, N.Y.: Prometheus Books, 1999.

Tassy, Pascal. "The Congolese Mokele-mbembe Report: Its Scientific Content. *Cryptozoology* 3 (1984): 136–137.

Weishampel, David B., P. Dodson, and H. Osmólska, eds. *The Dinosauria.* Berkeley: University of California Press, 2004.

WEB SITES

Hansen, Kathryn. "Dwarfing Earth's Largest Dinosaur." *Geotimes.* Available online. URL: http://www.geotimes.org/aug06/NN_dinosaur.html. Accessed October 5, 2009.

"Trends in Sauropodamorph Evolution." Available online. URL: http://www.kheper.net/evolution/dinosauria/sauropod-trends.html. Accessed October 5, 2009.

FURTHER RESOURCES

BOOKS AND ARTICLES

Barrett, Paul. *National Geographic Dinosaurs*. Washington, D.C.: National Geographic Children's Books, 2001.

Clark, Jerome. *Unexplained: 347 Sightings, Incredible Occurrences, and Puzzling Physical Phenomena*. Detroit, Mich.: Visible Ink Press, 1993.

Holmes, Thom, and Laurie Holmes. *Gigantic Long-Necked Plant-Eating Dinosaurs: The Prosauropods and Sauropods*. Berkeley Heights, N.J.: Enslow Publishers, 2001.

———. *Horned Dinosaurs: The Ceratopsians*. Berkeley Heights, N.J.: Enslow Publishers, 2001.

Marent, Thomas. *Rainforest*. New York: DK Publishing, 2006.

Novacek, Michael. *Time Traveler: In Search of Dinosaurs and Other Fossils from Montana to Mongolia*. New York: Farrar, Straus and Giroux, 2002.

Smith, Roland. *Cryptid Hunters*. New York: Scholastic, 2005.

Updike, John. "Extreme Dinosaurs." *National Geographic* 212 (December 2007): 32–57.

WEB SITES

Amargasaurus cazui
http://museumvictoria.com.au/melbournemuseum/discovery-centre/dinosaur-walk/meet-the-skeletons/amargasaurus/
The Web site of Australia's Melbourne Museum describes *Amargasaurus*, includes an illustration of the dinosaur, and provides a size comparison with the African elephant and an adult human.

Mokele-mbembe

http://www.trueauthority.com/cryptozoology/mokele.htm
Cryptozoological Web site TrueAuthority.com's file about
Mokele-mbembe includes a comprehensive list of expeditions to
the Congo Basin in search of the famous cryptid.

Mokele-mbembe: The Living Dinosaur

http://www.mokelembembe.com/
This summary of facts and figures about Mokele-mbembe
includes a bibliography and links to other Mokele-mbembe Web
sites.

Plate Tectonics

http://www.crystalinks.com/tectonicplates.html
This site presents an illustrated guide to plate tectonics. It
includes a cross-sectional view of Earth's lithosphere, showing
tectonic processes in action.

Who Dunnit to the Dinosaurs?

http://www.unmuseum.org/deaddino.htm
A good illustrated summary of the most popular theories about
what led to the extinction of the dinosaurs is highlighted at this
online museum.

PICTURE CREDITS

INDEX

ABOUT THE AUTHOR

RICK EMMER is a substitute science and math teacher for the Avon Lake City School District in northeast Ohio. He was previously an aquarist at the Cleveland Aquarium and a zookeeper at the Cleveland Metroparks Zoo. He has a bachelor's degree in biology from Mount Union College and a master's degree in biology from John Carroll University. He was a member of the International Society of Cryptozoology for several years. Emmer lives with his family in Bay Village, Ohio, smack dab in the middle of Cryptid Country, with the lair of the Lake Erie Monster to the north and the hideout of the Grassman, Ohio's Bigfoot, to the south.